The Martyrs of Malatya

Martyred for the Messiah in Turkey

James Wright
(pen name)

EP BOOKS

1st Floor Venture House, 6 Silver Court, Watchmead,
Welwyn Garden City, UK, AL7 1TS
www.epbooks.org
sales@epbooks.org

EP BOOKS are distributed in the USA by:
JPL Fulfillment
3741 Linden Avenue Southeast,
Grand Rapids, MI 49548.
E-mail: sales@jplfulfillment.com
Tel: 877.683.6935

First published 2015

British Library Cataloguing in Publication Data available

ISBN 978–1–78397–113–8

To give this book a more personal feeling and make it easier to read, it has been adapted into story form. While sources are referenced, parts of the story have been creatively dramatized while trying to stay as close as possible to the history and facts of the people and places involved.

Contents

The Martyrs of Malatya

Preface

On April 18, 2007, three men gave their lives for Jesus Christ. Two Turkish Christians and one German committed to taking the gospel to the country and people God had called him, began their day simply wanting to spend time with local men they thought genuinely wanted to study the Bible. Instead, five hostile young men met their kindness and hospitality with betrayal and treachery.

Very few followers of Christ in the rest of the world heard the story. Lost in the flood of news in our information age, it appeared to be just another senseless murder. But the deaths of Necati Aydin, Uğur Yuksel and Tilmann Geske, while perhaps ignored or quickly forgotten even among Christians around the world, continue to speak. They proclaim the truth that there are still those among us committed to witnessing to the gospel in difficult locations. They speak loudly of love for Christ and obedience to Him. They testify above the din about their commitment to share

Jesus' own experience of betrayal and sacrifice that purchased salvation for people from every tongue, tribe and nation.

James Wright has ensured that the three Malatya martyrs' stories continue to be told. Through *The Martyrs of Malatya*—already read by thousands in Turkey itself—Turks are learning of three men who genuinely loved them. James, through first-hand interviews of family and friends has carefully captured an accurate picture of these men, their families, their motives and their commitment in following the Messiah they loved. He has successfully put their story in the greater context of the challenge of spreading the gospel in Turkey and then also clearly demonstrates the hope we have for this land where the Apostle Paul first carried the gospel message two millennia ago. God is using this book to change lives and open hearts. It will do the same for you.

As the brutality of Islamic extremism and the death of larger numbers of Christians bursts through our social networking and cute cat videos, we have a tendency to brush off the deaths of unknown Christian martyrs with simple statements in a hollow echo of the early church father, Tertullian, "The blood of the martyrs is the seed of the church." May *The Martyrs of Malatya* help us realize that those who have given their lives for the sake of Christ are more than just unknown "seed"; rather, they are ordinary men and women who may have spouses and children. Yet, also, extraordinary men and women whose lives will convict all of us to follow Jesus wherever He leads—even down the road that leads to a martyr's crown.

Todd Jamison
International Mission Board, SBC
Central Asia

Introduction

Riding in the air-conditioned bus traveling briskly down the highway in eastern Turkey, I studied the dry landscape and quietly reflected on the events that had brought me far from the skyscrapers of modern Istanbul. I had an hour before the next stop so I thought back to the phone call I received three years earlier. That was the afternoon of April 18, when sitting in my home in Istanbul I got a call from a friend urging me to read the latest news on the website of a popular Turkish newspaper called *Today's Zaman*.[1] He sounded very upset, but didn't elaborate. I thanked him for calling and immediately opened the website. For the second time since 9/11 my body started trembling as I read the headlines: "Three Killed in Attack on Bible Publisher."[2] The first sentence said, "Attackers on Wednesday slit the throats of three people, including a German citizen, and caused one other to jump off a building which houses a Turkish publishing house which printed Bibles." My mind raced to my friends' office in

Istanbul as I imagined them lying helplessly in pools of blood. Scanning through the article I discovered the attacks had not taken place in Istanbul as I had first assumed, but to the east, in the heartland of Turkey. Five young men took the lives of Necati Aydin, Uğur Yuksel and Tilmann Geske.

Though I had never met the three martyrs, we had many mutual friends. A wave of mourning swept over me and hundreds of other believers who make up the tiny church in Turkey. After reading the article I withdrew into the basement where I could pray, read my Bible and weep. That's when I ran across Acts 8:2 where Luke narrates how the early church had just suffered the loss of Stephen. Refusing to leave his broken body in the public square, "some devout men buried Stephen, mourning for him with loud cries." I read the passage several times and asked myself, "What should we do when someone dies for Christ?" Here was the answer. We mourn. We mourn with loud cries. We mourn for the dead. We mourn for their killers. So I did … and still do.

On April 18, 2010 I joined many others in eastern Turkey to mourn and better understand the deaths of these three men. On the way back to Malatya after visiting Uğur's grave our tour bus sped past the dry hills and treeless crags. Every few miles we passed another small Turkish village consisting mostly of a few modest houses clustered around a market or two, a school and always a mosque. At Uğur's graveside a hundred folks, mostly Turkish citizens, made the grassy steppe resound with robust worship. In the distance, just at the edge of our view, the Turkish internal security forces watched over the proceedings. Whether to protect us from someone or protect someone from us, their automatic weapons made it clear they meant business.

Sitting on the bus I wondered, does anyone outside of these few Turkish Christians, some curious journalists and the alert security forces really care what happened on that ordinary spring day? Malatya is ten thousand miles from America, but could just as well be a million. Why should anyone care? In the bigger scheme of things, it's not that important, is it? The forlorn brown and yellow hills lining the highway mirrored my feelings.

The bus arrived in Malatya and deposited us all at the small Armenian graveyard where the Geskes buried Tillman after finally gaining permission from a reluctant local government. He was a German citizen, but gave his life for Turkey, so that's where his body should remain till the end. Again we gathered in a tight circle around the grave remembering Tilmann and giving thanks for his life. Locals living along the edge of the cemetery hung off their balconies casually watching the believers standing in the dusty field. What did they think about us disrupting their otherwise routine daily life of cooking, washing and sweeping? Later I learned that after the crowds dispersed someone entered the cemetery and intentionally damaged the new rose bushes Tilmann's family planted around his grave.

Standing at Tilmann's graveside I thought, this is where his Christianity got him. It got him a grave. Not a better job, not a bigger house, not inner peace, not success in life ... a grave, one that continues to be vandalized. He doesn't even get respect in death. This is the kind of story we would rather forget, not retell.

So then, why not just forget it and move on, especially since few people care anyway? That's what I wanted to do, just let it go. But then I remembered Stephen and his weeping friends. They didn't only mourn Stephen's death. They grieved the hopelessness of Saul of Tarsus and his kinsmen. Motivated and agitated by the murder, Saul made plans to arrest and murder more Christians. Facing such deadly persecutors, these guys obeyed the words of Jesus and prayed for their enemies.

Can such faith be found in the world today? Standing at the foot of Tilmann's grave, I had almost no faith, but what I had was just enough to believe it is not too late for us to re-evaluate our attitude toward Muslims, not too late to put our priorities straight, not too late to cry out, with tears and loud voices if necessary, for God to save even the most hate-filled, hardened enemies of the Gospel. Because I believe it is not too late for them—or us—I tell this story.

James Wright
Istanbul, 2013

1 No Turning Back

The young man brandished the knife in Necati's face and shrieked, "We're going to turn you back into a Muslim." Four other young men with knives moved in closer to the bodies of Tilmann and Uğur stretched out on the floor of the modest office. Uğur quietly whispered, "Isa ... Isa."

Necati strained against the cords that bit into his hands and feet, hoping to get a glimpse of his two good friends lying on the floor just a few feet away. His head throbbed from a hard blow and he fought to remain conscious.

Was this how it would end? He always knew that living for the Messiah in Turkey might also mean dying for him. The feet of his assailants shuffled around his head and their hideous laughter reached his ears, though the pain and wounds made them sound strangely muffled and distant.

Suddenly his body flinched with excruciating pain when one of the men pierced his abdomen with a knife and slowly turned it. He could hear more laughter and talking, mixed with groans he recognized coming from his friends.

Rapidly losing consciousness, Necati turned to see one of the young men wildly rummaging through his desk and stuffing his pockets. Uğur's cell phone started ringing. Someone shouted instructions for him to calm down and answer the phone. A faint bit of hope touched Necati's heart when he realized that someone outside the locked office had become aware there was a problem. The leader of the murderers ordered Uğur to tell the caller he was in a meeting in a hotel downtown.

One of the killers looked into Necati's face. Though he could hardly focus with his swollen eyes, he glanced at the familiar face of Emre. Just an hour earlier Necati had sat with the young man and his friends in his office. Uğur had served them all tea according to polite Anatolian culture while they exchanged courteous greetings and introductions and began to talk in a relaxed way about spiritual matters.

Necati and Emre had met several times in the past couple of months to discuss the meaning and message of Christianity. Coming from a traditional Muslim background, Emre had raised many questions in their prior meetings about the Bible, Jesus and Christian discipleship, but showing a level of interest in the subject that seemed more or less sincere if not overly enthusiastic.

Necati had talked to hundreds of his Muslim countrymen about the Messiah, going over passages of Scripture, comparing them to the message of the Qur'an, listening patiently to questions, objections and outright misperceptions, helping people get a sound grasp of the essential ideas of God's love displayed through the gift of Jesus the Messiah. Some had paid less attention than Emre had in their meetings and some more. When he did have moments of feeling uneasy about Emre's true motivations, he simply reminded himself that even someone with mixed motives should have a chance to hear the Gospel.

Sitting around the tea table earlier that morning, Necati was completely unaware of the real reason Emre had said he wanted to bring some new friends to a Bible study. After a few sips of tea and a few minutes of calm discussion, Emre started to become visibly agitated. Anger filled his eyes when he accused Necati of spreading a false religion and plotting to undermine the stability of the Turkish state. Emre's sudden change of mood heightened the tension in his friends. The room exploded with knives and fists and now Necati knew he was fading fast.

Finding comfort from somewhere deep inside, Necati thought about his wife. He thought about his children. He could see each of their lovely smiling faces. He thought about his Lord and Savior, for whom he had been called to lay down his life. He wept inwardly as he thought about the families and friends of Tilmann and Uğur; if only he could have done something to save them.

Yet with his moments quickly coming to an end, Necati felt reassurance that all was not lost. Holding steadfastly to his faith in the goodness of God he knew that he had not come accidentally to this final place in his life. He believed that long before he had ever heard of Jesus the Messiah and come to know him personally and powerfully, his life had flowed like a stream in the desert, not randomly, but all the way back to the very headwaters he had moved under the watchful and careful eye of God. No, they would not turn him back into a Muslim. He belonged to Jesus for eternity.

2

Three Sons of Adam

Founded on the vast plains of eastern Anatolia, the city of Erzurum has been a home for Turkish people five centuries longer than Istanbul. If any part of Anatolia captures the real spirit of Turkey, it's Erzurum with its deep sense of family, carefully observed traditions, religious piety and living in harmony with the stony mountains and grassy meadows. In the spring of 1972 the dry air of the East filled the lungs of the newborn Necati Aydin.

All Necati's relatives assumed that like everyone born in Turkey he was destined to be a good Muslim. Everyone was a Muslim and Christianity was deeply suspect. Under the leadership of Kemal Atatürk—founder of the modern republic—the Erzurum Congress of 1919 passed a historic document that would shape the Turkish worldview for generations. The fifth article said, "Christian minorities will not be permitted to break or divide our political sovereignty and our social balance."

Atatürk didn't trust Christians but he was likewise cautious about allowing Islam to run his country. Just a year before Necati's birth, the Turkish army, which considered itself guardians of Atatürk's vision, declared martial law and called for a reformed constitution in hopes of restoring civil order after an increase of agitation from leftists and religious Muslims. But the political discontent in the big cites in western Turkey made little difference to village folk. At sunrise each morning local bakers placed loaves of bread in hot stone ovens, sending a delicious aroma wafting down the streets and passageways of ancient Erzurum. So it was the day Necati arrived in Anatolia's cradle.

Through the summer and fall the healthy baby boy grew fatter and stronger. Necati was a sensitive little boy with haunting eyes; he enjoyed watching his older brothers and sisters playing under the boundless blue skies. In those first couple of years he grew on the bread and milk and yoghurt.

As the youngest of six children, he quickly learned the behavior of a Turkish boy. Before long he spoke his first Turkish words like *Baba* (Daddy), *An-ne* (Momma), *Abla* (Big Sister) and *Abi* (Big Brother). He listened to the sounds of Turkish folk music and watched the quick movements of the colorful dances. He awoke in the morning to the call to prayer sounding forth loudly from the nearest mosque. As an active little toddler, on some evenings he dropped off to sleep in the early evening before the last prayers. Everything going on in and around him was the rhythm of Erzurum ... the land of the grassy steppe.

One day when Necati was still very small his father announced they would move from Erzurum to Menemen, a city located on the Aegean coast, right in the midst of the ancient Seven Churches of Revelation. It was a long move but like millions from the East, his father needed work. Once settled into their new home Necati learned to enjoy life in the shadow of the nearby coastal mountains.

At six he donned his school uniform and trudged off to first grade. The little boy who still had striking eyes that sometimes seemed sad and searching joined in daily with his classmates to sing the Turkish national anthem and chant the pledge of allegiance, "I am a Turk, honest and hard-working!" He learned the history of the Seljuk and the long era of the Ottoman Empire. He learned how the Ottomans became the guardians of Mecca, Medina and Jerusalem, the most sacred sites of Islam.

Emphasizing the rise of the modern republic of Turkey, his teachers extolled the heroism of the First World War and the subsequent Turkish War of Salvation, when European powers had almost parceled out his beloved Anatolia. Like all good Turkish children, he felt proud to learn how Atatürk had risen to leadership at just the right time to turn back the foreign armies and bring a lasting deliverance and peace to Turkey, establishing the Republic of Turkey. Like his fellow students he memorized Atatürk's sayings, "How happy is the one who can say, 'I am a Turk,'" and "Peace at home, peace abroad." Being a sensitive boy, he sincerely wished to see peace in his world.

At the right time, Necati's family took him to an Islamic leader for circumcision. As Sunni Muslims, his mother and father prayed regularly, kept the fast, gave to the poor, made an annual sacrifice and in every way tried to fully observe the requirements of their religion. Their relatives and friends esteemed them for their devotedness to Islam. So it was perfectly natural that they should present their little Necati for the tradition of circumcision, marking him—for eternity they believed—as a Muslim boy and a Turk. His older brothers and sisters snickered at one another when a sore Necati had to rest in bed a few days after the procedure. But they knew that he was no longer a child, he had started his days as a young Muslim man.

Around the same time Necati's family migrated westward to the Aegean coast, another Turkish boy was born in the East in the remote town of Elazığ. On September 18, 1975 the Yuksel family welcomed their newest member and called him Uğur. Compared to so many other eastern Turkish cities founded on a rich and ancient history, Elazığ was a newcomer. In the 19th century the Ottoman government made Elazığ a military and administrative center. It grew in modern Turkey with industrial and agricultural production and an important university was founded there in 1966.

That Uğur grew up in the shadow of a university seems fitting because he was always a deep thinker. His parents encouraged him to study and question. They were happy he had opportunities they didn't. Uğur was quick with languages too. Like many of his neighbors, he could speak good Turkish and Zaza. He liked to read, though finding books in Elazığ in the post-military coup of the 1980s was not easy. There was no internet; for that matter, most homes didn't have a television. Those that did could only choose between a handful of government channels. Still, Uğur managed to inquire about the larger world near him and beyond, always curious about what more was out there, just beyond the plains and hills and mountains.

As good Alevi Muslims, the Yuksel family made sure that Uğur was raised with the knowledge that there is one God. At the right time they presented him for circumcision, permanently identifying him as a Muslim and as a man. Uğur continued to grow taller and leaner, quietly loving his family, making friends and serving his country. He showed competitive aptitude in his schoolwork, passing tests and earning good marks, so it became apparent that he would be able to attend the university. For some people the university becomes a place of wrong decisions or time wasted. For Uğur, as he would explain years later, the university gave him a safe place to make the most important discovery of his life.

Few places in the world overflow with as much lush green summer foliage as Germany. On July 18 1961, while Germans struggled to rebuild after the devastation of WWII, a family in Mindelheim, Bavaria gave birth to a strong son and called him Tilmann Ekkhart. The lovely summer weather welcomed his parents onto the green lawns so the sunshine could warm Tilmann's face.

The same year Tilmann was born, Germany welcomed the first wave of 7,000 Turkish guest workers into their country to help them rebuild. That same year the Communists started erecting the massive Berlin Wall, the concrete symbol of the wide separation between Eastern and Western Europe. The West Germans, with a reviving economy, desperately needed a larger labor force. They made an agreement which allowed Turkish guest workers to come and stay longer than two years, opening the door to hundreds then thousands of Turks. Not only could workers come, but later laws allowed their family members to join them, giving West Germany the highest population of Turkish guest workers in Europe. While thousands of Turkish guest workers poured into his homeland, Communists poured cement in Berlin and Russian soldiers erected machine gun posts along hundreds of miles of border, the innocent Tilmann took his first baby steps.

But the big events didn't trouble him. His family enjoyed the fact that after two horrific wars claimed the lives of millions, their country had finally taken a turn toward a more peaceful existence, one where they could safely and securely raise their little boy. So Tilmann, like all good German children, headed off to school to develop his special intellectual gifts, his musical talent and his quiet social nature. By the time Necati chewed his first piece of soft Erzurum bread, Tilmann was already a strapping youth, strumming his guitar and dreaming about all the adventures he would see someday as a grown man.

Three boys with three very different pasts … yet they shared a common humanity. Blood flowed red in each of their veins. In each of their hearts God's image generated creativity, intelligence and the awareness of right and wrong. Each little boy would grow day by day facing a difficult road that stretched like a shimmering thread to the distance days of adulthood. Not one of them could foresee how his individual path would carry him—one from the Aegean coast, one from the Anatolian steppe and one from the green fields of northern Europe—to a common friendship and a common destiny.

As the days passed and they grew to maturity, each one in his own time and way began to sense something was not quite right with the world around and the world inside. Sometimes they found themselves doing the very things they didn't want to do, or not doing the things they wanted to do, falling short of their own standards. The resulting moral disappointment and inner spiritual anxiety would send these men on a quest. The answers for their troubled hearts would not be quickly or easily discovered. Their search would take them down many valleys and over many mountains before leading them to the place of final peaceful trust. Their paths would also bring them to an ultimate fiery trial forever forging their brotherhood.

Two Sons of Turkey

Necati's mother tried in vain to subdue the stubborn shock of black hair on his head as she instructed him about having his picture taken at school. "Now stand straight and tall," she said, reaching for his collar. "*Mashallah*, you are a good boy. Now go, it's time to leave already." Necati smiled at her, "Yes Mother." He loved his mother and father and family and always wanted to please them. Today would be no different. He obediently slipped on the dark blue smock and the bright white collar. Necati looked like any one of a million Turkish children heading to school. He gathered up a few things and said goodbye to his family.

Everyone at the crowded public school was excited on picture day. The girls wanted to look their best and a great many of the boys tried to look their worst. A cacophony of shouts, screams, laughs, cries and conversations filled the dusty schoolyard. Necati tried to keep his uniform tidy, so he avoided playing with the rough kids. Necati liked numbers so he enjoyed sitting in the math lesson with dozens of other kids, trying to hear the teacher explain how to add and subtract Turkish Lira when buying eggplant and peppers in the bazaar.

At mid-day his teacher rounded up the seven-year-olds and explained how to get in a line and wait for their photograph. Necati naturally complied with no complaints, even though the boy next to him continually stuck his tongue out at him hoping to get him into trouble. Finally his turn came to stand in front of the camera. He felt embarrassed about the fuss made over a photograph. But he knew his family wanted a nice picture, so he forced himself to stand still and present a pleasant expression. Some days later the photos arrived. His parents took them out eagerly with endless *Mashallah*s expressed to ward off the curse of the evil eye. Surely this bright-eyed little son of theirs was headed for some kind of special future. They recited their prayers and best blessings over him.

Uğur's neighbor had just gotten a new television, one of the first in the village. Now a young adolescent he enjoyed hanging out with his friend watching whatever they could find, which usually wasn't much. It was mid-evening, so his friend's mother was preparing supper while the boys passed time watching a couple of cartoons followed by a Turkish film. A young actress caught his eye; she was a pretty girl, probably just a few years older than Uğur. There were a couple of pretty girls in his class at school, but none who looked as cultured and well groomed as the girl on television. He felt a twinge of embarrassment when he thought about the physical changes he was going through. Although some of the boys at school joked quite freely about girls, Uğur never felt comfortable with that kind of talk. He was far too conscientious to join the crude behavior he saw in some of the other boys.

As he sat quietly his thoughts turned for a moment to a neighbor girl he had noticed recently. He had known her since primary school but never thought much about her until now. Suddenly he realized how he enjoyed watching her stand huddled with her friends in the schoolyard each morning, talking and laughing as girls will do. He turned to his friend who had just come back from the kitchen with a bowl of apples and said, "Hey, you think you'll ever get married?"

"What?" his friend said, dropping down on the sofa, "I'm just hoping I survive my military duty, I don't think about anything beyond that. Here, have an apple." He offered Uğur the bowl and said, "What got you thinking about that? Is there a love story on TV or something?"

Uğur took the apple and smiled, "Oh, I don't know, I guess it's just something I'll have to think about sooner or later." He took a bite of the juicy apple. His friend laughed and said, "Later … more like it. Maybe your parents will pick out a nice girl for you anyway, so you won't have to worry about it. Don't you have some decent cousins?"

"Yeah, maybe. I just hope it is somebody I love."

His friend punched him on the shoulder and laughingly

replied, "The hard part will be finding some nice girl who loves you."

Necati sat outside under a dazzlingly bright starry sky. He had grown much since the day the school photo captured the image of a timid little boy in a blue smock and white collar. His physical frame was still on the lean side, but hard work with his brothers had started to build his muscles. He sat alone under the night-time sky that evening, having waited patiently for the sun to set westward, over the Aegean Sea, painting a spectacular display of colors. Necati gazed toward the heavens, feeling particularly small under their expansiveness. He had no problem believing God must exist, with such an awesome display of creative power stretching overhead. But somehow he felt lonely. The family house was crowded with several brothers and sisters and loving parents, but there were still times he felt alone. Necati's dad, who was over sixty, showed affection to his youngest son, but whether from lack of time or energy, his elderly father was sometimes unavailable.

Time passed and more stars popped out in the inky sky. He wondered about his future. The high hopes of his parents and siblings filled the house like their noisy conversations. It would be an honor for the clan if one of them could become a religious scholar. As devout Muslims, his family could see that Necati possessed the aptitude and the pedigree to become such a leader. As a mosque leader he could not only continuously study the Qur'an, Hadith and other religious writings, he could teach others and earn a living doing so. The option seemed attractive. He wanted to help people and he wanted to serve God. If this was the life-path God had written for him, he would gladly take it as a thankful slave. For one last time before heading to bed he paused to soak up the starlight.

"Really, Uğur was a philosopher," a friend said, recalling long conversations with him. Maybe it was something about the windswept hills of Elazığ where Uğur was born and grew up that instilled in him an abiding desire to understand the mysteries of the great world around him. The air of eastern Turkey is thick with centuries of people seeking to understand spiritual things. The ground is heavy laden with massive stones used to build empires that have come and gone since the dawn of time. Noah's ark rested somewhere in the craggy mountains and Abraham, the father of monotheism, had walked the wide, fertile plains of southeast Turkey and lived in the settlement of Haran. His example of faith established a pattern of life repeated by people over and over for centuries. Uğur was one of these seekers, looking carefully into things of the past to discover truth to shape his future. During his schooling he had become well acquainted with Marxism and Buddhism and added the study of those systems of thought to his native Alevi Islam. A man with a peaceful nature, he believed in working for social justice but eschewed violence and radicalism.

Late nights in the coffeehouse kept him close to the table with friends discussing philosophy. He couldn't find intellectual satisfaction in atheism while he wrestled with the most basic questions of existence like what is the purpose of life, why are we here and who is God? Uğur spent hours with friends sipping tea, smoking cigarettes and contemplating the possible answers to these questions.

Sometimes the discussions grew quite animated. He quickly learned that almost any option was open to discussion. He could imagine ways to harmonize the mysticism of the Far East with his native Alevi Islam, imaging that all humans had come from God like drops from an ocean and at death all would melt back into the divine ocean. He believed that Allah or the Ultimate Reality, whatever he could call him, was the origin and destiny of all humans. But beyond that he could say little about him. The tea and coffee flowed, the conversations intensified, but there was one topic few dared to broach: Christianity. That was simply too much even for his intimate band of free-thinkers.

After the Friday sermon Necati left the mosque and his friends. They wished each other well and encouraged one another to remain faithful. Later in the evening the time of prayer came again, so he went to the washroom to do his ablutions. Allah wanted him coming to prayer spotless and pure, but since the last Namaz he had already allowed himself to linger several minutes too long in front of the television watching a program from the West with its shameful images. He could see why some Muslims called the West the Great Satan. Wasn't the West like Satan, with its love of money, sex and power, sending its seductive whispers throughout the world, drawing people, even many Muslims, away from the straight path? He felt unclean and tricked, therefore he took great care performing his washing again, trying to prepare his body and mind for coming before Allah in the prayers.

In this way Necati continued to advance in his Islamic faith. His sensitive nature and strong conscience compelled him to wash and pray five times a day, rarely missing. He wanted to be clean, truly clean, he wanted to be forgiven and made right in the sight of God. Even his family took note of his unusual piety. But deep on the inside questions nagged at Necati. Could he ever be truly clean? Could he ever know for certain God's forgiveness? Could he ever truly reach heaven? How could he know for sure? Was there any guarantee? He had often said that Allah is merciful and oft-forgiving, but there was always the risk that he had one more sin, one more unclean thought or action that would bar his way to heaven. Perhaps after eighty years of pious living, Allah would still find him unacceptable and send him to hell. The questions nagged, the fears assailed, so he increased his devotion more and more. He resolutely determined to become the best kind of Muslim a person could be ... *Inshallah.*

One day after Friday prayers at the mosque, Necati joined a friend for tea. His friend spoke excitedly. "You have to see this Necati. Here's the writing of a clear thinker, the kind of leader we need in the Muslim world today. Look at this." He put a booklet on the table for Necati to examine.

After reading for a few moments Necati asked, "Who wrote this, it is quite intelligent?"

"*Hoja* Fethullah Gulen." His friend answered. "There's lots of good material here, look at this paragraph." He pointed to the middle of the page and started to read, "In the recent past, the Islamic world as a whole has lived through its most depressed periods, whether considered from the point of view of faith, morality, modes of thought, education, industry, customs, traditions, or practices."

Necati stopped him, "I couldn't agree more, we have fallen so far …"

"Yes, listen, it gets better," his friend said, continuing to read:

Yet once Muslims were far more distinguished in their piety; they were more devout, more correct and decent in their morality, more stable and wholesome in their customs and practices, more worthy to dominate world affairs on account of their social and political horizons and their more progressive and sophisticated modes of thought. They practiced their religion without fault or failure, perfected their morality, understood the place and value of science and knowledge, always managed to be ahead of the level of learning and the standards of the era in which they lived, and properly appreciated and balanced the relation and interaction between inspiration, reason, and experience …

Necati sighed, then added, "*Vay vay*, there must be a way to recover the past honor."

His friend smiled and said, "Yes, I think that the *Hoja* is the kind of leader with vision and ability capable of helping us recover the lost glory. Let me continue,

That is why they were able to rule such vast lands, from the Pyrenees to the Indian Ocean, from Kazan to Somalia, from Poitiers to the Great Wall of China, with the best administrative and governing system known up to that time, and their ideals aroused the admiration of all. While other peoples were experiencing the darkest ages in their history, the Muslims, in the territories under their jurisdiction, enjoyed and extended to other

peoples systems of governance that were idealized as a utopia or an
earthly paradise

"What a wonderful thought," Necati said after sipping his tea.
"Imagine ... if we could work for the return of Islam at its proper
place in the world, how much more just and fair the world would
be for all its citizens. But how did we get into such bad condition
anyway?"

His friend frowned and said, "We have to face the problem to
find the solution. Here's what the Master *Hoja* says, 'What a pity
that this part of the world deviated and distanced itself from the
historical dynamics and Islamic values which had kept it standing
upright through the ages, and that it became slave to ignorance,
immorality, superstition, and carnal pleasure. This is when
Islamic civilization began its slide into the abyss of darkness and
great disappointments; when it began to be dragged into one
crisis after another; when it became scattered everywhere, like the
beads of a rosary when the string has been snapped; when it was
left under the stairs, like pages fallen from a book with a loose
binding.'"

"Perhaps we can help gather up the scattered pages of the book,
I would do what I could for my part" Necati said.

"As shall I," his friend replied, "and there is hope, listen:

Despite many efforts of ill-meaning detractors, from within
and without, the recent gloomy period has in fact not lasted long.
Muslims today, who now account for about a fifth of the human
population, are striving for a fresh revival nearly everywhere in the

Islamic world and are trying to save themselves from this accursed era of enslavement. Particularly in recent times, the fact that they have had to face new calamities every day has heightened the spiritual attentiveness of Muslims, has given momentum to their return to God, and has aroused and excited their resolve. And today we are able to witness, in all walks of life, a fast-growing inclination to Islam; we can now observe that Islam is coming to the fore and gaining prominence in a vast area, from the United States to the Asian steppes, from Scandinavia to Australia.

His friend paused to sip some tea, then added, "Just think Necati, there is a great movement globally, a movement for the truth, and we are part of it."

"It inspires my heart to imagine it," Necati said, smiling at his friend.

The friend continued reading;

Although many missionary activities of different faiths are systematically carried out by various groups, they have been unable to arouse one tenth of the interest and warmth in their respective religion that greets Islam. Today, throughout many continents of the world, thousands of people choose to embrace Islam every year, taking refuge in the light of the Qur'an, even though they know that they may be sentenced to some form of starvation and misery. Unless we fail to keep our loyalty to God, glad tidings of the divine message will be experienced once more.

"And then there's this:

From America to Europe, from the Balkans to the Great Wall of China and the heart of Africa, indeed, almost everywhere, faith, hope, security, and therefore, peace and contentment will be experienced once more under the umbrella of Islam; the whole of humanity will witness a new world order that is far beyond imagination; everyone will benefit to the extent to which their nature, disposition and mentality allow.

His friend stopped reading and took a deep breath. "There it is. Isn't this amazing and wonderful, a vision of Islam rising to its proper place at the helm of the world, taking its rightful role as the foundation of all human society, bringing a new age of order and justice for all peoples everywhere? The time has come for such a revival of the true faith!"

Necati sat quietly for a few moments, replaying the words of the respected Fethullah Gulen. Here was someone offering a picture of the future free of oppression, exploitation, violence, and all kinds of immorality. It was a vision he could believe in and live for. Finally he spoke. "Yes, the world belongs to Allah and Islam, not any other religion or philosophy. Here is where we can find our hope."

Bus Ride to Eternity

Reaching early adulthood Necati took a job in the nearby city of Izmir, requiring him to take lengthy bus rides through the mountains. He didn't mind them so much, they gave him time to think, something he enjoyed doing. One day he hopped onto the crowded bus like any other day, expecting a normal trip, standing up and hanging on while the bus careened around sharp curves and over steep hills. But that day was different, vastly different. It would become the day his entire life changed for all days and forever.

Necati paid for his bus ride and began making his way to the back, expecting to look in vain for a place to sit undisturbed on the long ride. To his surprise and then disappointment, he noticed an empty seat. He was surprised because he rarely saw an empty seat. He was disappointed because next to the empty seat sat a young lady. She did not have her head covered and she was reading a book. But with more people sure to get on at the numerous stops ahead, he decided in a split-second that it seemed comfortable and safe enough. It was the only empty seat, and though he was conscientious about keeping his honor with women, she seemed absorbed in her reading, and they were on a public bus after all, so he took the seat.

Necati enjoyed asking questions and he had an irrepressible curiosity. Seeing a woman on a bus reading a book, rather than playing with a cell phone, staring aimlessly out of the window, flirting with a boyfriend or glancing through a women's magazine at glamorous models made him curious. It was no small book, but had hundreds and hundreds of pages with small print. He glanced out the window and down the aisle, trying to ignore the book and the woman reading it. The bus bumped over potholes and uneven pavement, kicking up dust. Still she read, unfazed. He glanced over at the book, trying to determine what it was. It was written in Turkish, he could see that much. He could also make out the word *Tanri* (God) here and there. At last, unable to keep silent, Necati said, "Excuse me, I don't mean to be rude, but I noticed you reading that book."

The woman looked up and smiled, a pleasant smile, not frightened and not flirtatious, just a peaceful smile. She said, "Yes, I read often and I have lots of time on the bus."

Necati wondered for a moment what the woman thought of him, sitting there with his impressive full, black beard, a sign of his commitment to Allah. Evidently she didn't seem to think anything negative, at least she didn't show it.

He said, "May I ask what it is you are reading?"

She replied, "Of course, it's the *Injil*, the New Testament".

Necati recoiled instinctively. The Bible! This woman was a Christian, he felt repulsion. But after his initial reaction, he still felt curious. He had seen some verses from the *Injil* here and there in his religious studies. Hesitatingly, he said, "Are you ... a Christian?"

"Yes, I am."

This was probably the first time he had ever met a Christian. Here was his chance to set one straight. He said, "But the Bible has been changed. The Qur'an is the final revelation."

The lady studied him for a moment; surely she must have noticed his beard and his conservative clothing, indicating his commitment to Islam. "I don't think the Bible has been changed," she said gently. "It is God's Word, and he would never allow anyone to change his Word."

Never in all his life had anyone spoken so directly with so few words challenging Necati's beliefs. Of course everyone, absolutely everyone, knew that the *Tevrat*, *Zebur*, and *Injil* had been changed. There simply was no argument, case closed, discussion over. Yet here was this young lady on the bus seated next to him, reading the Bible in Turkish.

She continued, "I wonder, have you ever read the Bible?"

Lying or exaggerating weren't in Necati's character, so he answered honestly, "No, I've seen parts of it here and there, but I have never actually read it. For that matter, I'm not sure I've ever seen a whole copy of the Bible."

"If you really want to know the truth, then you should look into the matter more deeply for yourself. Don't just go on what you have heard others say, get a copy of the Bible and study it for yourself," she said.

The young lady made sense. How could he be prejudiced? Furthermore, in many verses, the Qur'an commended the Bible. He nodded his head slowly. "I suppose you are right," Necati replied.

"If you want to know God, you need to seek for him, that's what it says in the Bible—if you seek, you will find."

"I do want to know God, I mean, I want to know his straight path, the path of truth and righteousness."

"Then I would recommend to you to read and find out for yourself," she said. She looked up, "Well, I see my bus stop is coming soon. Have a good day."

In the days that followed their initial meeting the regular bus ride brought their paths together often, giving them many more opportunities to talk about spiritual matters.

One day on the busy bus Necati saw her and smiled politely. "Hello," he said, "how are you today? I suppose I should introduce myself. My name is Necati."

The young lady returned his polite smile and answered, "I am Shemse. Pleased to meet you."

"I'm pleased to meet you. Oh, by the way, I've been reading the *Injil* since we last talked."

"Good, I'm so happy to hear that. And what do you think of it so far?"

"Well, you know I told you that I have always heard it has been changed. I have read through the testimonies of the four writers, Matthew, Mark, Luke and John. Okay, there are some differences here and there between them, but only very minor points, and the differences are vague, maybe someone who could read the records in the original Greek could work out a clearer understanding."

"Have you enjoyed reading them?"

Necati smiled, "Yes, very much, somehow ... it's really not like anything I have read before. For example, take the teaching of Jesus on the mountain. He seemed to have a completely different attitude about love and hate than most people in the world. Like saying that we should love our enemies and forgive those who mistreat us, and his remark that if someone strikes our cheek we should turn the other one to them. I mean, the ideas are wonderful, if we could just live like that the world would have peace between peoples."

The bus started to slow down. Shemse said, "Sorry, I must go now. Have a good day."

Necati shifted in his seat. "Actually I have some business in this part of town today ... perhaps we could talk a little more as we walk?"

"If it's no problem for you, of course," she said. "We can talk a bit more."

"No, I would appreciate it," Necati answered, exiting the bus with his friend.

They continued their conversation walking along the road. "There is so much good in the Bible," Necati said, "but still, I have been told so many times that Christians have everything wrong. People say the Bible has been changed, the original Bible lost and Christians believe in three gods."

"Now that you are reading the Bible for yourself and we have talked, what do you think? You're entitled to your own opinion, aren't you?"

Necati paused a moment, thinking carefully about his answer. "I can understand the accusations, but the more I study they seem to be describing an imaginary situation. Okay, I know that some people light candles and pray in front of paintings of Mary and Jesus and Christian saints. That could be interpreted as worshiping Mary like a god. And I've heard some people call Mary the Mother of God. But I haven't found anything like that in the Bible itself. Perhaps it was a tradition that developed sometime much later after the period of Jesus and his disciples. And another thing I discovered when I was reading the book *More Than a Carpenter*, the earliest copies of the New Testament come from the first and second centuries. The earliest remaining copies of the Old Testament predate Jesus. Hundreds of these ancient copies were carefully written to avoid mistakes in the text and were preserved. Hundreds of earlier copies match copies from the third, fourth, and fifth centuries and so on."

"So," she asked, "could they have ever been changed?"

"I don't see when or how they could have been changed. I don't see who could have changed them. The result is that the Bible existing at the time of Muhammad is the same as the Bible of the 1st and 2nd century and the same as the Bible we have today. There has been no change, I mean, the Bible is not changed. And the Qur'an also clearly points people to study the Gospel saying in chapter 5:47, 'Let the people of the *Injil* judge by what Allah hath revealed therein.' Another interesting point is that the Dead Sea Scrolls discovered in the 1940s in a cave confirm the accuracy of the modern copies of the Old Testament. The book of the prophet Isaiah they discovered dates back more than 2000 years, making it the oldest copy of an Old Testament book in existence. The modern copies of Isaiah match this ancient copy with amazing accuracy. And in any case, I just can't help but wonder why God wouldn't protect his Word and allow mere humans to corrupt or destroy it."

"Do you remember the verse I showed you from the New Testament? It says, 'All human beings are like grass, and all their glory is like wild flowers. The grass withers, and the flowers fall, but the word of the Lord remains forever. This word is the Good News that was proclaimed to you."'

"Yes, that's exactly my point, how could God reveal his holy word then allow it to become corrupted and changed by the whim of man. Wouldn't God protect his message?"

Shemse smiled, "Yes, I think he would."

As time passed a conviction began to grow in Necati's heart. The more he studied the Bible, the more his confidence grew that these were not the words of some heretics who had changed the original *Tevrat*, *Zebur* and *Injil*. These were the same words that Moses had written regarding the earliest days of time and humanity. They were the same words David had penned when he was a shepherd inspired by God to write beautiful poems and songs of praise. These were the same words Jesus had spoken during his sinless life upon the earth. Necati began to realize he could chose to ignore the story but he couldn't dispute it.

One day Necati and Shemse sat together drinking tea and talking. He returned his tea cup back to its dish and said, "But I'm still having a very hard time understanding what Christians mean when they say God is one in three. Isn't it just another way of saying that Christians worship three gods?"

"Remember what John said, 'In the beginning was the Word, and the Word was with God, and the Word was God. The same was in the beginning with God. All things were made through him; and without him was not anything made that has been made ... And the Word became flesh, and dwelt among us (and we beheld his glory, glory as of the only begotten from the Father), full of grace and truth.' You could think of it like a person, who has his thoughts, feelings and a will. We can express our thoughts, our words, they come out of us and are part of us, but we can also express them, by communicating them to others."

"But even this verse from John calls Jesus 'begotten of the Father.' This goes against everything I have ever been taught. God is one and he has no equal, no partner, and no son. To suggest otherwise is blasphemy."

"Yes, it would be blasphemy if Christians suggested that God has an equal, like a second God. But that's not what the incarnation means. It doesn't mean God had a wife and they had a son. It means that God himself came to live among us in a human form."

"But this sounds like Christians are saying Jesus and God are the same."

"John 10:30 records Jesus saying, 'I and Father are one.'"

"So you are saying that Christians do not believe God had a physical son? That they believe that God miraculously took a human body and lived on the earth? But it is so hard to understand how the all-powerful God who reigns supreme over the entire universe would debase himself to the degree of taking a human body with all the natural bodily functions and temptations. It doesn't seem possible!"

"Just don't forget Necati what the *Injil* says, 'With men this is impossible; but with God all things are possible.' Jesus never acted contrary to the nature of God. He never sinned, he never showed any dishonor, he did miracles and healed people and in the end he rose from the dead, never to die again. Who else but God can do these things?"

"But, why? Of course with God nothing is impossible, but it doesn't seem likely. Why would God go through all that? He didn't need to."

"Because he loved us. He didn't need to, but we needed him to. Scriptures says, 'For God so loved the world that he sent his only begotten son that whoever believes in him should not perish but have everlasting life,' and 'But God demonstrates his own love toward us, in that, while we were yet sinners, Christ died for us.' There is no other answer but love."

Necati sipped his steaming tea, pondering the words of the *Injil*. Could it be that divine love motivated God to come in a human body and dwell among men, in the exact form of a man? Part of him wanted to believe in such amazing, personal love, but it seemed almost too good to be true.

As he thought about Jesus, the amazing person whose life he had studied intensively these past several weeks, he began to feel ashamed. Jesus had lived a sinless life, but Necati thought back over his own life, it was not sinless. He could remember the wrong things he had said, the failed efforts to live up to a high standard, and the uncertainty about all his efforts to please God.

Shemse could sense a shadow fall across his face as he thought about it. "Is something the matter?" she inquired.

"I was just thinking, I could never deserve such a great love. If God loved me so much that he would visit our world in the Messiah Jesus to face humiliation, suffering, and death, I could never repay him. I know my own heart, and it isn't worthy."

Shemse laughed, a very pleasant sound to Necati, and said, "But Necati, that's the whole point, you don't have to be worthy of God's saving love. Jesus gives it freely. He died on the cross in your place as a sacrifice. You need only receive him."

"How can he take my punishment? No man can take another man's guilt. If I sin, I alone must face my own punishment?"

"Like the Scripture says in Romans 5:9 and 10, 'much more then, being now justified by his blood, shall we be saved from the wrath of God through him. For if, while we were enemies, we were reconciled to God through the death of his Son, much more, being reconciled, shall we be saved by his life.'"

Necati saw a flicker of light in his understanding. "So the *Injil* says that Jesus took the punishment for my sin. It's like Jesus fulfilled the law for me and took hell for me."

"Jesus was the perfect sacrifice, the lamb of God, sacrificed in your place. The work is finished."

"Okay, someone can believe in Jesus, but then couldn't they go out and continue to sin and just say they have nothing to fear any longer since Jesus has forgiven them? Isn't this like a license to wickedness?"

"Absolutely not, the Apostle Paul said, 'What shall we say then? Shall we continue in sin, that grace may abound? God forbid. We who died to sin, how shall we any longer live therein?' Once a person comes to the Messiah, everything changes. Once someone has come to truly know the light they should no longer want to continue in the darkness."

Necati sat back in his chair and said, "Yes, I think I see your point."

"You know, I meet regularly with some other believing friends … I would like you to meet them, if you wish."

"Yes, I would like that, let me know when we can meet."

"There's a meeting next week."

"Let's go then, meanwhile I'll keep studying, maybe I can ask more questions at the meeting." Necati glanced at his watch. "I'm sorry, I have to be getting along, but thanks for your time, I really enjoyed it."

The next week Necati joined the small but friendly meeting. The believing Turkish people sang simple songs of praise to God in their heart language, worshipping humbly as followers of Jesus. They uttered prayers, though not in any particularly formal way or in a foreign language as Necati was accustomed to doing in Arabic. When some of the group shared some health concerns and their need for God's assistance in difficult relational circumstances, someone else prayed from the heart about the problems, as though talking to a very loving and interested father. The whole thing made a deep impression on him.

Surmounting the Obstacles

In 2010 a close friend of Necati named Dogan discussed the kinds of hurdles that a Muslim like Necati must surmount to become a true follower of the Messiah. For example, is it a sin according to Islam for a Turkish Muslims to read the *Injil*, the Christians' Holy Book? "It's fundamentally not illegal nor a sin," Dogan says. "First of all, the *Injil* is a legal book and I can't imagine it being a sin because even Muslims have in their faith the teaching that the *Injil* was revealed from heaven. However much people may say that it has been changed, there's no such thing as the original, the idea that it's illegal or a sin is not true."

Was Jesus a Westerner? "Jesus Christ was an Easterner; he came into the world in the Middle East, lived in the Middle East and gave his life as a sacrifice on a cross in the Middle East for the entire world. The good news about Jesus Christ went out from the Middle East to the lands of Turkey then spread westward. It's not that the message came from the West, it came from these lands and went to the West."

What about stories like *The Da Vinci Code* that imply Jesus was the creation of Greek Gnostics. If a Turk or Middle Easterner— it doesn't matter, Alevi, Sunni, secularist or whomever—is interested to learn more about Jesus, what should they know? Dogan thinks, "Because Jesus Christ gave his life on the cross as a sacrifice for every Turk, each one has the right to know and learn about this. If someone gives his life for you and you aren't aware of the sacrifice he made, this would be a very frightening thing to lose. Whether or not a person accepts, every person has a right to hear and make his or her own personal judgment about the matter."

Is there a cost for following Jesus? "Yes, there is a serious cost to pay, especially among our people. Necati, Uğur and Tilmann and others like this paid the price. They paid the price of following Jesus with their own lives. But for that matter Jesus Christ said to his disciples, 'if they treat me this way, what will they do to you?' He said that in this world his followers would have much trouble."

During the entire time of searching and examining the faith of the Christians, Necati had refrained from talking about it with his family. He couldn't exactly predict the extent of their disapproval, but he knew that reading the *Injil* was risky, that they might react very strongly if they found out. The more he considered his options, the more he became convinced that if the Gospel were true, that is, if he could truly receive eternal life in Jesus Christ, the reward for trusting in him was greater than any risk he might face with his family.

As with all loyal Turkish young men, the time came for Necati to serve his country in the military. The army trained him and sent him to Northern Cyprus where he gained respect from his commanding officers for honest, diligent and intelligent service.

While in conscripted military service he stayed in touch with Shemse and his friends in Izmir. He also continued his quest to find the truth, often thinking and praying, asking God to show him the true path of freedom that would take him from a life of sin into abundant and eternal life with God.

The time in Cyprus away from Shemse also gave him space to think about their relationship. Over the weeks and months of talking together, first about spiritual matters, then about general life, their relationship had slowly grown in appreciation and friendship. Now that he was away from Izmir on the island of Cyprus, he would gaze across the dry hills, carefully considering all the implications of the possible changes he faced. Was he willing to follow Jesus? Would he follow Jesus with or without Shemse? Were his motives pure in regard to the question of following Jesus? What if Shemse shared his emerging romantic feelings? Would it be fair to ask her to face the pressure and possible rejection they might both face if they married? His background as a traditional Sunni Muslim and hers as a traditional Orthodox Christian could mean problems with both their families. Suppose it created tension and conflict between the two of them? But their faith in Jesus was not just based on their families' traditions; they had each personally put their faith in the living Christ. Of course their backgrounds were much different, but the differences had been minimized in Jesus who served as a bridge between them, a point of common commitment. During their separation while he lived on Cyprus Necati wrestled with the questions but came to have a peaceful reassurance that he indeed loved Shemse and wanted her to be his wife, but that if she didn't share his feelings he would still continue in the way of the Messiah Jesus.

The army discharged Necati after his required period of

service, giving him an excellent report for having well-served the Republic. Once back in Izmir, Necati eagerly sought out Shemse. He had made up his mind and would not look back. Whether or not she agreed to marry him he had decided to follow Jesus. Earnest talks with friends confirmed that he had soberly evaluated what it would mean to be born again in the Messiah. It was clear that even though he loved Shemse, his faith in Jesus was sincere. He wasn't a fake or a pretender just hoping to win her affections and he had no plans of trying to make her become a Muslim. Of course she had influenced him, ever since he first saw her reading the Bible on the bus. But he interpreted this to mean that God had used her as an instrument to help him find Jesus.

What if something went wrong and they broke up? Would he likewise renounce his faith in Jesus? He would not want to face a painful separation from her, but to the best of his knowledge, he could honestly say that he would follow Jesus with or without Shemse. With confidence that his faith was true and permanent, Shemse happily consented to marriage proposal.

After he made his decision to follow Jesus, the small group of believers in Izmir rejoiced greatly with him at his baptism. Like countless Asians, Middle Easterners, Europeans and Africans throughout the ages, Necati went under the water as a sign of his death with Jesus the Messiah then burst up out of the water as a sign of his resurrection with him. All gathered around smiled and sang and celebrated that his old life had passed away and he had become a new person in Christ.

Some people who have an independent or rebellious

personality never give a second thought to what their family might think about their choices and behavior. Some actually seem to enjoy making their parents and siblings angry and ashamed at the things they say and do. Such had never been the case with Necati. His heart ached over the angry reaction his family made to his faith in Jesus and his engagement with Shemse. He wanted to somehow help them understand so that if they didn't at least come to agree with him, they would still be friendly.

It didn't happen.

One of his brothers was a religious teacher in a city on the Black Sea. His family forced him to go to his brother, hoping he could get Necati to renounce his Christian faith and return to Islam. The pressure mounted. On occasion they threatened his life. How could he possibly bring such shame and dishonor upon them? How could he, of all people, with his training in the Qur'an and his deep devotion as a youth give it up for a religion everyone considered blasphemous? In their eyes he was a traitor. Necati tried to demonstrate patience, love and kindness as evidence that he hadn't betrayed his family or his country. By then he knew well how to answer the arguments that Christians worship three gods and the *Tevrat*, *Zebur*, and *Injil* had been changed. While being able to defend his faith in the Messiah, he didn't want to disparage his family's religion. That wasn't his purpose. He wanted to speak about the love and joy he had found in Jesus the Messiah, though it was hard at times to avoid becoming argumentative. However, his family persisted in their pressure to persuade him to give up his faith, so he spent less time with them, a decision that nearly broke his heart.

Joyful times came in 1999 when Necati and Shemse married. He took his wedding vows most seriously as he made a commitment in his heart to love Shemse no matter what, until death would someday separate them. Friends gathered around the young couple, sharing in their obvious love for one another, offering to stand by them in support. Though few spoke of it, most were aware that his marriage choice and faith in Jesus had cost Necati a peaceful relationship with his family.

The competitive Turkish job market didn't readily hand the newlyweds good jobs. In his adult life Necati worked in a variety of contexts, including keeping accounts for a compressor company and a confectionary company that made Turkish Delight. He had aptitude in math, computers and management, skills that he would draw upon in his future ministry. They put their wedding together with a very meager budget, though the warm presence of their church family and their contagious joy at being finally together in marriage made it a beautiful event. After praying earnestly about the need for cash to cover wedding and honeymoon expenses, Necati and Shemse received an unexpected package one day containing just enough to cover their needs. Years later when reflecting on the miraculous ways God had worked in his life, Necati would often mentioned that miraculous wedding money.

Not long after their wedding, the Zirve Christian publishing and distribution company started seeking reliable new workers and Necati had caught their attention. Fondly remembering his first impressions of Necati, one leader said, "If I had to pick out someone who I think most embodies who Jesus was (chuckles) Necati embodies a lot of that. He had a really compassionate and tender heart for the Lord ... yes it was really clear that everything of who he was, he was ready to give in service of Jesus. And he loved his kids and his wife and yet had a determination to get into ministry, to get the Word out.

With his background as a pious Sunni who had come to believe the truthfulness of the *Tevrat, Zebur* and *Injil,* Necati could bring fresh insights and abilities to their company. They could see he had much potential for clearly explaining the contents of their books and other publications and for eventually giving effective leadership in the organization. Necati was a Turkish man who represented his people in their sociology, psychology, language and culture. He had carefully and honestly investigated religion and philosophy, so he was able to think in a new way, yet he understood and loved his people and country so much. He wasn't angry or suspicious about other people. He had a unique way of seeing value and potential in every individual and believed that everyone should have the opportunity to study and discover just as he had. He wanted to give his countrymen the same opportunity. This made him a sort of unique bridge, just the kind of person Zirve needed for their publishing and distribution enterprise. In 2000 Zirve formally invited Necati to come work with them.

Uğur ...
Personal

Uğur started his spiritual journey from an entirely different place and time than Necati, but the steps he took eventually led them together as best of friends. In a Christian radio interview broadcast in Istanbul, Uğur and Gul talked about how he found in Jesus the Messiah the peace and hope he had longed and searched for since his days on the steppe of eastern Turkey.

After settling comfortably into the studio chairs, Gul and Uğur waited for the signal. Gul smiled, welcomed Uğur warmly and then started her questions. "Tell us about yourself."

Feeling a bit nervous, Uğur started with the basics. "I was born in 1975 in Elazığ. Because of changes in my father's work, we moved to Diyarbakir and I was a student in middle school and high school there. We moved back in 1993. My family had four children."

"All right," said Gul, calming Uğur's nerves with her easy demeanor, "during those years, what kind of understanding did you have of God or a creator and how to have a relationship with him? Or did you feel a need for something in your life that you began to search for?"

This was the kind of question he loved discussing and the words poured forth. "I never rejected the idea of God. I tried to be an atheist because my friends were atheists, but I never was. I come from an Alevi background, so I probably had it easier with my family never telling me 'this is your God and this is your Book.' But of course my family was an example of morality. I always believed in the existence of God from just the way I saw how this world is perfectly made."

"So how did your story develop about your coming to have an encounter in your life with the living God?" she asked.

"As I said, my family never put pressure on me to believe any certain way. I'm a person who loves to read, and as much as I had the power to do so, I started reading everything I could, like books on Buddhism, Hinduism, monotheism and polytheism. I also investigated my own background of Alevi Islam. I was an Alevi in name and I knew that I had that in my background and why I had come to have that in my passport as my religion. As I studied it I concluded that I could say it wasn't what really described me."

"You read much about other religions and were affected by your search so that you saw that your Alevi identity didn't really describe you, and yet you didn't deny the existence of God, so where did this road really take you?"

Uğur eagerly answered, appreciating her probing thoughts. "I can say that after that, I always enjoyed reading, but I didn't enjoy the studies I had to do for schoolwork. I finished middle school and then high school in 1993 but waited nine years before I took the university entrance examinations. During those years I didn't take any exams. I think it was in 2001 my family said I should just take the university exam, and since I didn't have anything to lose, I registered to take the exam. My first choice for college was Kocaeli and I won a place there studying construction. So I went to Kocaeli where I read lots of books. One day I was sitting with a group of university friends when a professor came by and sat down with us. The subject turned to religion. I mentioned that I believed in a creator of some kind, but that none of the books I had read about religion offered anything that I thought was true. At that point the professor suggested I read the *Injil*, though I don't think he was personally a believer. I didn't talk to him very much, but I think he was an atheist and looked to Jesus as a sort of philosopher with wise teachings. He asked if I had every read the *Injil*, and I answered that I had never read it nor been able to find a copy, but that I would have read it if I had ever found a copy.

Gul seemed genuinely surprised. "Of all the books you had read, you never read the *Injil*?"

"Never. I never read it, but I had the notion that Christians believed in three gods and that the *Tevrat*, the *Zebur*, and the *Injil* had been corrupted over time, these ideas were just things I had heard passed along to me by word of mouth. If someone had asked, I couldn't have produced any evidence that the Bible had been changed. At that time I was living in a prefabricated house built for earthquakes and I had an Injil sent to my home there. As I look back, I can say that I read through the entire *Injil* three or four times within a week."

Again Gul visibly expressed amazement and replied, "If it had been a typical book, you wouldn't have wanted to read through it more than once."

"This normally would have been a difficult thing, but something kept drawing me back to the book. I had to read it again and again, especially the book of Matthew, where I found in Jesus' sermon some ideas that changed some of my earlier thoughts which I had from the philosophies of Haci Bektas and Mevlana. I didn't see God physically, but I knew that God never commanded and could never command war."

"His character became fixed in your mind?"

Uğur paused for a moment, looking for the right words, "I mean, I could say that it was like a blueprint sketched in my mind. The Sermon on the Mount comes across not exactly as a law, but as a spiritual foundation, an entirely new model, or I could say what God wants from a perfect person. And here's something else very interesting that happened when I was reading the *Injil*, something came back to my mind. You see, one time long before I started reading the Injil, I said to myself, 'I am a true child and one day I will find my father and live with him.' Even my friends knew that I had said that to myself and sometimes they laughed about it."

Nodding with understanding, Gul said, "So it seems that these words or this sentence, which is in harmony exactly with the Biblical concept of becoming children of God, was not something that just accidently came to your mind, but was planted in your heart by God before you ever read the Scriptures."

"Yes, it was a theme that I heard inside, that I was a son and one day I would find my father and live with him. When I read the *Injil*, I discovered that Jesus said, 'I am the way, the truth, and the life.' It was like God said to me, 'You have sought me, if you want to come to me, here I am,' like he was speaking to me personally. The time came I found him as I had sought him, and as I said, the Sermon on the Mount in the *Injil* and many other places in the *Injil* were placed in my mind like a sketch."

She smiled and said excitedly, "That is a wonderful answer; and I suppose that you made a decision at that moment? I mean, what did you think about your understanding of having experienced God's Word shared with you personally?"

"After reading the *Injil* quickly through, from Friday to the next Saturday if I'm not remembering incorrectly, I knew in my mind and heart that this was the truth I had been seeking and that yes, absolutely, I had no doubts, God was the source of this divine invitation, and I can look back and see that this was God's choice."

"Can you explain what changes you saw afterwards?"

"I didn't meet with anyone one to one, but afterwards I confessed my faith to others, but as I said, I had already believed in my heart. I began to understand why God had brought me to that university in Kocaeli and I went back home before finishing school."

Gul leaned forward a little and said, "When person looks back on the steps he has taken living in the way of God, you can see the changes and what a difference it makes that they are developing for a purpose, and how these steps are put together walking together with the living God."

"After I went back to my home, for example, among the Alevi, we hadn't given much value to worship or religiosity, because we considered ourselves to be honest, decent people. Like the tax collector story told in Matthew, we thought, 'sure, I'm an honest man, I don't need these things,' but as I get closer to God, I see how sinful I am, or how deceitful I am, like getting closer to a bright light shows how filthy I am. When I told a lie, I could say to myself, 'when a person is not speaking the truth, he is influencing only himself.'

"Of course, we could also say that whenever we lie, we aren't really hurting anyone else. But compared to the glory of God, we all fall short, and when we examine our lives, we see the importance of this truth."

He smiled and answered, "In time God taught me the spiritual truth that in whatever circumstances, whatever difficulties, however others react to difficulties, I shouldn't respond in the error of falsehood. Also, God taught me how to live with pain and hardships, though I had reacted at times in a natural way with tears."

She nodded, "This is a very important thing you've said. We live in an enormous cycle, we receive God's blessings upon us, but then after having a day like a pink rose we face great tests, problems and sufferings. We aren't overcome by the world's hardships because as you said, God uses everyone to strengthen us and we work in his power to overcome. Okay Uğur, how is your life going now and what are you doing, because God isn't one who shows himself to us and then leaves us, but is someone who lives with us every day and never lets us go, so how is your relationship going these days?"

"In 2003 I returned to my home and opened a communications business working for about two years but then problems forced me to close it. For six months I went through a very difficult time financially, but even more than that, I went through a really hard time spiritually. But I thank and praise God that through this hard time he showed me how I need to trust him and live in his grace and cast myself upon him. Then after that, by his grace I began to work for a publishing house. Working with him in this responsibility under his blessing is really a high honor."

Gul laughed and said, "Even as you spend time working, you aren't spending a moment away from him."

"Sharing and explaining him is certainly a wonderful thing."

Determined to Go

Tilmann stepped off the airplane, stiff from the long flight back to Germany from Indonesia. He knew he would never be the same. Very little in his hometown reminded him of the tropical island nation of Indonesia. He had walked their streets, teaming with throngs of people traveling about on every conceivable kind of transportation: bicycles, carts, taxis, trucks, cars, foot. Though he was back in the tidy, efficiently run German society he could not shake the impressions formed during his trip to Indonesia. His mind replayed the muezzin crying out the call to prayer that echoed across the vast city, summoning the faithful to put aside whatever they were doing and remember their Creator. The exotic sights and sounds and smells of the open markets with their fresh fish stands, the jostling shoppers looking for a bargain to feed their hungry children and the endless streets lined with merchants vending their wares contrasted sharply with the quiet little Bavarian bakery on the street corner in his village.

Yet even more deeply than the allure of the cultural novelty, Tilmann felt drawn to the Indonesian Muslims. He had observed their piety, their families, and had gotten a taste of friendship with them, something that he cherished. Along with the friendship that had started to bloom when he drank tea and chatted with Indonesian friends, a love and compassion for them had taken root. He could see their smiling faces in his memory, lovely people with the same kinds of hopes and dreams, pains and sorrows, and yes, short-comings and sins that he experienced in his own life.

Still a bachelor, Tilmann could sense the loneliness and frustration that many of the Indonesian bachelors must have felt while they often tried in vain to find work sufficient for them to support a future wife and family. Not being able to find a job left them in a perpetual state of singleness, wishing for the companionship of a young woman. And though he sometimes felt lonely, he felt that somehow life wasn't quite fair, because he knew he could easily get work in Germany and he trusted God would bring him the right kind of wife.

He could also look around at the prosperous German society and reflect on how soft and easy life was for his own countrymen, while millions in Indonesia struggled to provide adequate medical care and other basic necessities for their families. He realized that the comfortable life he and his family enjoyed in Western Europe hadn't always existed. In his grandfather's lifetime two world wars had torn Germany apart leaving cities in utter ruins and society without hope. Yet they had rebuilt, reconciling with old enemies and cooperating with new friends, like the Turkish guest workers who had started arriving in Germany the year of his birth. At first hundreds then tens of thousands of immigrants came to provide the much needed strong backs and arms to put Germany back together. While the German people had prospered in the post-war years, the Turkish immigrants had also prospered, sending great wealth back to relatives and friends in Anatolia. Tilmann considered it a good thing they had blessings so abundant they had more than enough to share.

But what could he personally share? After all, he was just one person and the people of Indonesia numbered in the millions. Not only that, but he felt a special love for all Muslims from every place, and they numbered over a billion. What could he as one man do? Now, firmly grounded in his decision to follow Jesus, Tilmann prayed and studied, looking to him for answers to his questions.

One day after his return from Indonesia a friend dropped by to visit.

"How are you, Tilmann," his friend asked, sitting down with him in the café. "I haven't seen so much of you lately?"

"I'm well, thank you. I have been busy since returning from my trip though."

"I think that trip must have made a big impact on you. Tell me about it."

"Ah, where could I begin? It was an amazing thing. So many wonderful people, so many challenges and opportunities ... I wish somehow I could be of service in such a place among such a people."

"Do you mean among the developing nations?"

"Not only just that. I believe God would want me to somehow give my service to Muslim peoples. I think I have a place in my heart for them."

"But you are a Christian Tilmann and they are Muslim, the differences are too many, I think. Don't you?"

"Yes, many differences, but many similarities as well. And I believe that somehow we can cross over the differences and find a place where I can communicate with them about God's love."

"I admire your faith, for that matter, I always have. But it will be difficult. There are so many centuries of misunderstandings, so many conflicts, so many disagreements. How will you cope with all this?"

"Of course there will be difficulties, Jesus spoke of this, '... blessed are those who are persecuted because they do what God requires; the Kingdom of heaven belongs to them.' Jesus prepared us to take up our task, to be like salt to the people of the earth, but he makes it clear that it will not be a task void of hardship."

"Yes, I see your point. Still, there are so many people whom you could serve even right here in Germany. Why can't you just go to other Christians or to people who are historically Christian? Many Germans and Europeans have lost their way too Tilmann. They have lost their faith and hope in God."

"Sometimes I wonder the same thing, that perhaps God could use me here. It is true that many have lost their way; many have lost their faith and hope in Christ. Yet for those who wish to find their way back, many qualified men and women already live here who can serve as a guide. Are there not people who have less or even no opportunity to hear the message of Jesus? Millions walk the streets and alleys of Jakarta who have only the slightest knowledge that a man named Jesus lived many years ago. They have no Bible within their reach and no hope of ever having God's word in their own language. Their only idea of a Christian is a drunk, immoral person, or a violent, greedy oppressor. Perhaps I can show them that the way of Jesus is wholly different. Perhaps I can be like salt to them, bringing a new and life-giving flavor."

"Ah, Tilmann, we have been friends a long time! You have such a kind heart. I will tell you openly, you are one of the most honest, faithful, good-hearted people I have ever known. I know you well, but what if the Muslims you meet see you differently? What if they misinterpret your intentions? They may think you have no right to speak of your beliefs to them. After all, they have their own religion and seem contented with it. Some of them have been Muslims for a thousand years!"

"Thank you for your kind words, and your concern. I know you are only thinking of my best. And I think you have legitimate concerns, these are questions I sometimes ask myself. Am I presumptuous to think that I have something to offer? When in Indonesia I saw that I have much to learn from my Muslim friends. They love their children, take care of their relatives and neighbors and treat their guests with generous hospitality. They are some of the finest people I have met. But in the final analysis, I know that I am not the judge. I know that we can't judge ourselves against one another."

"What do you mean?"

"For example, near my village lived a man known to drink heavily and abuse his family. Close by lived another family who always showed love and kindness to each other and the villagers. Compared to the drunken man, the second family seemed very good. But how do we each compare to God? You know what scripture says, 'For all have sinned and fallen short of the glory of God.'"

The friend paused, and then asked, "But does that really mean everyone who ever lived? I mean, maybe the upright family you describe really hasn't sinned, certainly not like the drunk man."

"God does not judge like man does. He looks on the inside. If God looks in every person's heart, he will see the stain of sin, in some it is darker perhaps, and in some lighter, but still we all stand with shame before God. Our good works, our religion, our best behavior can't conceal it forever."

"In that case, what does God require?"

Tilmann paused for a moment, drawing his breath. He

answered, "I believe what Jesus says, 'I am telling you the truth: those who hear my words and believe in him who sent me have eternal life. They will not be judged, but have already passed from death to life.'"

His friend leaned forward and said, "Are you saying then that even the Muslims, though they believe in one God and speak of Jesus as a prophet still need something more?"

"I believe that God wants to give them something more. He wants them to know his abundant love through the Messiah that he sent. That's why I believe I should go to them, as a messenger of this eternal life in the Messiah Jesus."

Some weeks later Tilmann saw his friend again. They greeted each other warmly and his friend said, "I heard the news about your new job, driving a forklift in the warehouse, congratulations."

"Thank you. That's not all. New Life church in Lindau has asked me to help them. I will teach and do some administration. It's a new church and has potential. I think it is an opportunity that the Lord has given me in preparation for the work I hope to eventually do in another country."

"I am truly happy for you Tilmann, and I believe this is an important step in your life. New Life church is fortunate to have you join their leadership."

Tilmann blushed at the complement and said, "I praise God for the doors he opens, I want to be faithful to walk through them obediently."

In the months following, Tilmann worked diligently driving the forklift, not always an easy or safe job, but he worked skillfully earning a good reputation. The warehouse job was part-time giving him the rest of the week to serve people in New Life, a small church of fifty people. True to character, Tilmann took both the church and warehouse work seriously, considering both jobs a way to glorify God in his life.

One morning Tilmann and his co-pastor got a phone call that would alter his destiny. A young woman named Susanne had recently finished Bible college and needed a church where she could volunteer as a intern. Her teachers described her as enthusiastic and eager to share her faith with others. After Tilmann and his friend talked and prayed about the situation they decided to invite Susanne to come and help the church. She agreed, quickly packed her things and moved to Lindau. When she arrived in town she found a job working for a wholesale business, riding to work each day on her well-worn bicycle.

The first day Tilmann met Susanne, her vivacious personality impressed and intrigued him. She was younger and had been a Christian fewer years than he had. But her enthusiasm to serve Jesus made up for the difference in their maturity. Tilmann, a very quiet man, felt awakened in the presence of this lively, talkative, new college graduate.

Susanne eagerly wanted to know how she could serve New Life, but Tilmann thought that she needed to get settled and let the church get to know her better. When they told her to wait, she seemed obviously disappointed. A few weeks later she came back to talk to the pastors.

Sitting on the edge of her chair Susanne opened the conversation, "You know, I'm really getting used to being here now, and I've been looking around for ways to serve because I feel that's what I should be doing of course."

"I can understand," Tilmann said. When he spoke, which he didn't often do, it was always with a very quiet voice. Susanne concentrated to hear what he said as he continued. "How is your accommodation? I apologize it isn't any nicer."

"No, they're fine, really, it doesn't matter to me if I have something luxurious or not. They are clean and modest and safe, thank you. But what would really make me happy is doing something productive for the Lord."

"Yes, well … uh, did you have something in mind perhaps?"

"Actually, I noticed that New Life doesn't have a bookstore. I could gather some good reading materials, things that would encourage people and help build their faith. You know such a thing could be very useful. So tell me, what do you think?"

Tilmann sat for a moment, then answered, "I think you are exactly right. We need good reading materials available for the community. We will do whatever we can to help you."

They talked and started making plans for Susanne's idea of providing books for the church members. After the meeting Susanne left feeling re-energized. When she left the room the other pastor turned to Tilmann and said, "I think she will be quite an asset to the church, don't you?"

Tilmann thought a few moments about Susanne then said, "Yes, I agree."

Within months Susanne's impact on the church and the village of Lindau had grown. The nature of their work with the church meant that Tilmann spent lots of time with Susanne in all sorts of contexts. Sometimes they sat together during a church prayer meeting. Other times they met to discuss a special project or ministry plans. He saw her each week during the church's regular worship and teaching times. The more time he spent with her, the more he wanted to spend time with her. He was aware, painfully aware at times, that her personality brought color and sparkle and zest into his dull, brown and gray world. He felt that she complimented him in a marvelous way and that on the other hand, he had gifts of stability and steadfastness that could benefit her. Sometimes he wondered what she felt about him, but at that point he was too cautious and shy to ask.

Tilmann's co-worker saw Susanne one afternoon at the church having a cup of tea. "Hello," he said, "how are you?"

"I'm well, thank you," she answered. "Would you like a cup of tea? I'm just resting a bit. Tilmann and I had to rearrange the classroom this morning."

"Yes, I would like a cup, thank you," the pastor said, sitting down. "Tilmann is a hard worker isn't he?"

Susanne squirmed a little, she wasn't sure she wanted to talk about Tilmann, but she answered, "Yes, I suppose so, I mean, he is quiet and all, but he does get a lot done."

The pastor chuckled and said, "Doesn't the old proverb say, 'Quiet waters run deep.'"

Susanne sipped her tea, trying to think of a way to change the subject, but she couldn't react quickly enough.

"You know," he continued, "Tilmann thinks very highly of you."

"He thinks highly of everyone in the church and in the village. That's just the kind of person he is."

"Yes, well, he cares for all, but I know for a fact that he has taken special notice of everything you have done since you came." He paused, chuckled again and added, "he's taken special notice of you."

Susanne reached for the sugar, "Would you like some for your tea?"

"I can't think of a much better guy than Tilmann, one of the finest I've ever known," the pastor said, looking at Susanne, trying to gauge her reaction.

She shifted in her seat and said, "Everyone in New Life is just great, I've enjoyed getting to know everyone."

"Of course, but not all are eligible young men with lovely character and personality."

"That's true, but really, Tilmann's not for me, I mean, we're just so different and …"

The pastor laughed and set his empty cup on the table. "Yes, well, sometimes opposites attract. But I must be going now. I'll tell Tilmann hello from you."

Tilmann's friend may have felt free to tease Susanne, but Tilmann was very quiet, unable to express his growing feelings of fondness for her. Susanne temporarily left Lindau for a camp several hundred kilometers away, giving Tilmann time to search his heart. He decided he must say something to her about his feelings. Tilmann was good with written words. He knew English and had learned New Testament Greek at college. Writing his thoughts and feelings always came easier than trying to say them aloud, so he sat down one day and wrote her a letter. He wanted to take the risk of telling her he cared for her and wanted to get to know her better … to learn how she felt about him. When she returned to Lindau, Tilmann was disappointed and surprised to learn she never got the letter. It had been lost in the mail. He would have to try to work up his courage to talk with her directly. He would wait for the right opportunity.

Weeks passed, during which Tilmann and Susanne spent more and more time in a variety of ways. Some mornings they shared breakfast at the church. Tilmann wanted to learn more about what made this interesting young lady tick, so he asked questions, trying to draw her out on a deeper level. On occasion he let Susanne use his car so she could get to her new job at a pottery factory. Still, he didn't know how she felt about him. The day finally came he would find out.

Tilmann drove Susanne home one afternoon. Just before

getting out of the car, she turned to him and said, "I have something to ask you."

Tilmann looked at her, trying to force the words to come out of his mouth, "I have something to ask you too."

"Please, could I borrow your car tomorrow?" she blurted out, looking a bit embarrassed, perhaps from having already borrowed it so many times.

"Yes, of course, I mean it's no problem, I don't mind at all. Really."

Susanne looked relieved. "Okay, so what about your question? You said you have something to ask me, what is it?"

Tilmann hesitated, started to speak, then stammered, "I, uhh, I wanted to ask, uhh, I just wanted to know, uhh."

Susanne interrupted, looking at her watch, and said, "Tilmann, I need to get on and pack before I go away …"

Tilmann saw he must come out with it. So he looked directly in Susanne's eyes and uttered, "Do you want to marry me?"

In a rare moment, Susanne sat speechless; they both sat looking at one another in silence. Finally she answered, "Okay, I have three conditions that any potential husband needs to fulfill. One, you have to be a believer; two you have to have been a believer longer than me; and three, I want to live in a Muslim country."

Tilmann smiled and his eyes lit up. He answered confidently, "Oh, this is fine with me! Ever since traveling to Indonesia I have known I must eventually move back to live among Muslims. This is a special calling God has put in my heart. I have always seen my ministry with New Life as just a step in preparation to give my very best when the time comes to live among my Muslim friends. This is something I have wanted to do, even before I met you Susanne. But it is something we can now both share."

"I wouldn't want you to do this just for me," she replied.

Tilmann answered, "Of course not, you have become the most important person in my life, but God is still higher. I will follow him."

They talked much longer. Susanne agreed she would pray and fast in the coming week about Tilmann's proposal, promising to give him an answer in seven days. A week later she answered as promised. It was the answer Tilmann longed to hear, "Yes."

On December 26, 1991, Tilmann and Susanne become formally engaged. Susanne wrote in her journal,

> God knows me through and through. He knows everything that I need, better than I know myself. Thank you Lord, for giving me Tilmann. I consider him as coming directly from you. I would like to place this relationship under your protection and ask what you would like, even in this area …

> Thank you Lord, for Tilmann. He is a great comfort. Thank you that you have given me a view of what is to come, for that

was just the beginning. It will be a steep and bumpy road, but with a clear goal before our eyes. Lord, I thank you for Tilmann. I am so pleased that you granted him his wish for a wife. We are getting to know each other bit by bit and are discovering how to work together. It is clear that we are very different but it is fascinating how much we have in common. Lord, I see your work and guidance, Thank you that Tilmann wants to marry me. I can barely imagine what it will be like but I am so happy. I have a real deep peace about it. Yesterday he told his mother and I told my mother about it: Oh Lord, I am so happy! I love you Lord. Amen[2]

Tilmann took Susanne as his much-loved wife on June 20, 1992. Once married, Tilmann and Susanne kept alive their hope of someday living among Muslims to share the message of eternal life in Jesus Christ, but they didn't know exactly where they would move. Would it be Indonesia, Iran, Turkey or some other place? They prayed and talked, trusting the Lord to direct their steps in his time. During their honeymoon they visited Istanbul. On a boat ride one day near the city they noticed a traditional Turkish family riding next to them. Tilmann was impressed how the Turkish parents lovingly attended to their children. Perhaps God wanted them to someday live among the Turkish people? He later commented to Susanne that he could picture them living in Turkey.

In time other circumstances arose confirming to Tilmann and Susanne that Turkey was the place for them. Tilmann contemplated how he could offer a useful service to his Turkish friends. He decided that his language skills qualified him to teach English, so he finished his training in teaching English as a foreign language and began making plans to open a business in Turkey. It would require much hard work, but Tilmann was completely committed to do whatever he must to become a friend and servant of the Turkish people. Before moving to Turkey Tilmann and Susanne gathered with friends who encouraged them with a verse from the Bible. It said, "You did not choose me but I chose you and appointed you to go and bear fruit—fruit that will last."

Tilmann purchased a used van in Germany from a Turkish family, packed it full of belongings and headed south with his family. He and his oldest daughter took ferries and drove while Susanne and their son flew, all destined for Adana on the Mediterranean coast.

Life on the Mediterranean was very different to anything in the cold clime of Northern Europe. Yet they worked hard to adapt so they could meaningfully build relationships with their Turkish neighbors and friends. Having exceptional linguistic skills, both Susanne and Tilmann made quick progress in speaking Turkish. Tilmann took a job teaching English, but sometimes found it frustrating when the students didn't progress as quickly as he wanted. Not one to give up easily, he persevered in doing his best to serve and live as an example of a true follower of Jesus the Messiah.

The Geskes became acquainted with other foreign believers in the area. They were eager to meet together for Christian fellowship and worship. At first they met in a home but later found a rented building that both an international church and a local Turkish group would jointly use. Tilmann enjoyed contributing to the church by putting his carpentry and draftsman skills to work remodeling the building.

Making friendships and raising their family in Adana proceeded without many problems, but Tilmann and Susanne had a desire to someday move further east where they could live in a more traditional Islamic community. One day while gazing at a map of Turkey, Tilmann took special notice of the city of Malatya. It was further east in the heartland of Turkey, the kind of place he wanted to live. It also had a university, which might give him the kind of relationships to start his own language business. As a pioneer and entrepreneur, he felt intrigued by the possibilities. Unbeknownst to him, Malatya had come up in a conversation between Susanne and some friends and she too had felt very curious about it. When they learned of their shared interest in Malatya, they decided to visit in 2002.

7 National Scandal and Prison

Known as the most tolerant and progressive region of Turkey, the Aegean coastline provided many opportunities for Necati to develop his skills in communicating the Gospel meaningfully and accurately. Orhan,[3] his first partner in the Zirve Company, would become one of his best friends during four years of experiencing the joys and pain of their shared ministry.

The two men traveled widely through the ancient land of Asia Minor, sometimes tracing the very steps of the Apostle Paul. During their two and three day excursions outside of Izmir (formerly Smyrna), Necati and Orhan distributed a great quantity of Christian material such as the New Testament, the Jesus Film, and books, all in Turkish. They visited tea houses and markets, mingling freely with local people; looking for any opportunity they could find to express the good news. Along the way they met a wide spectrum of responses, some positive, and some less so. On more than one occasion men from the various tea houses complained to them that distributing Christian material was illegal, though in fact the Turkish law did not prohibit their activities. During one trip, some local men took their complaints to the Turkish internal security forces, called the gendarmerie, requesting they do something to stop them.

The gendarmerie enthusiastically responded. They shadowed the believers for hours then decided to set up a road block in order to arrest them. When they stopped the two believers, they took them into the police station and informed them about the complaints against their work. Police showed them a document that men from the tea house had signed, accusing Necati and Orhan of slandering their religion and their prophet. Necati and Orhan were fully aware that the statement had been fabricated and later learned that the complainers had been coerced into signing the false document as a pretext for charging them.

Hours passed and the police made no sign of releasing them. The late winter weather at the time of their arrest turned colder, so some believers from Izmir who had learned of their arrest drove out to the station, bringing their coats and some food. The press also learned of their detention, most likely from the police, and showed up in full force. Officers moved Necati and Orhan into the press room; someone placed their identification cards on a table in full view, allowing the press to photograph their personal information, endangering them. Under the portrait of Atatürk on the wall, the gendarmerie made a spectacle of Necati and Orhan, as if they had apprehended two highly dangerous criminals. National television and newspapers immediately broadcast the story, suggesting the believers posed a subtle and serious threat to their country and religion.

With the two men standing accused, the courts ordered them to be sent to a prison for thirty days while their case would be examined further. In the small prison, Necati and Orhan struggled to make the best of their trial. When feeling anxiety about his wife and children, Orhan reminded himself of God's word, that God loved his family more than he loved his own children. In the overcrowded prison cell, filled with many curious men, Necati and Orhan began sharing their hope.

To help Necati pass the dull hours and add joyful music to his witness a friend brought him his saz, the seven-stringed folk instrument of Anatolia. After becoming a believer, Necati had learned to play the saz. He once said, "since we are a Turkish church, we need a Turkish musical instrument, we need the saz, not just the piano and guitar." During the thirty days of imprisonment they spoke with fifty men. The small national church rallied around the two persecuted believers, visiting them continuously at the facility and securing reliable legal counsel. As days passed many across the Turkish nation and around the world prayed for their release.

After thirty days of incarceration the men received hopeful news. The courts dropped the case—they could go free. When packing their bags on the last day, the head warden recognized the exemplary behavior of the believers. He had quietly watched their words and conduct and come to the conclusion that they were upright men. Instead of demanding they open their suitcases for the customary final search, he waved them on, showing respect not usually bestowed upon the guilty men under his watch.

Necati and Orhan rejoiced to be back with their families and friends. With the law on their side, they resumed their work for Zirve, traveling over the hills and through the forests of the Aegean region. In a sign of forgiveness and reconciliation, they went back to the tea house and visited some of the men who had been coerced into accusing them of insulting Islam. The meeting was peaceful, stirring at least one of the former accusers to visit the church in Izmir.

In Search of Hassan

How could two ordinary men from the western Turkish coast where most people boasted of their tolerance become embroiled in a national scandal that thrust their story before millions and land them in prison for several weeks? Their only crime was distributing the New Testament and other Christian material. What created the immense store of negative energy that fueled the outrage against them? How far would people go in their hostility against Christians? To explore these questions requires a trip back in time to the days of the Ottoman Empire.

Just east of Istanbul stretch out the lush, green plains of Adapazari. For longer than anyone can remember, Turkish villagers have raised vegetables, fruits and livestock in those fertile fields nourished by the mild Black Sea climate and abundant mountain water. At harvest time they brought their produce to the town of Adapazari to sell in the open markets, arriving weary and hungry. Many of them found a friend or a relative who could give them a hot meal and a place to rest their body, jarred from the long roads winding down from the mountain villages. Others had no close friends or relatives nearby, so they would look for a *han*, or inn. During the Ottoman days the Turks and Armenians had separate quarters of Adapazari. They lived according to the traditions of their ancestors, asking few questions, desiring little change. But unusual developments had opened the door for strange ideas.

Sometime around 1846 a man called Steppan traveled from Adapazari to Istanbul in hopes of finding treatment for an enlarged liver, having had malaria. He spent the night in Izmit, halfway between the two cities. Travelers relied entirely on their own feet, horses or carriages, so the journey from Istanbul to Adapazari could take days. Word quickly passed among the guests that a couple of Protestant missionaries were also staying there. That news caught Steppan's attention. He hoped they might have some medical skill to treat his disease, so he found them and introduced himself. Yes, they could recommend a medical treatment for his physical problems, but they wanted to give him something more. It was a gift, the New Testament, recently translated into modern Armenian. Steppan respectfully and gratefully received the medical treatment and the book.

After his trip to Istanbul Steppan made his way back to Adapazari and began to excitedly show his new Bible to friends and neighbors in the coffee-shops. Some of the customers at his small business lingered to chat more about the book. It was the first of its kind, as far as anyone knew, to reach Adapazari. Even though the Armenians considered themselves Christians, they knew virtually nothing about their own Holy Book. Men in town wanted to know more, so one of them went to Istanbul in search of more books and materials. After carefully reading the Bible and the other new books, some of them decided to follow Jesus. Similar things happened in hamlets across the empire. In response, the Armenian Orthodox Church Patriarch issued the *Great Anathema* (Great Curse).

In the Armenian section of Adapazari the power of the Great Anathema quickly mobilized almost everyone against the new believers. Mobs formed and attacked their mud-brick houses, pushing them down with the sheer force of their hands and numbers. After destroying three houses they came to one built of timber and stone that proved impossible to push over.

The house stood on the border between the Armenian and Turkish sections, so the uproar aroused the attention of some Turkish women watching from their windows. They shouted "See what they're doing to the Protestants because they don't worship pictures! Well! We don't worship pictures! Next they'll be after us!" Like a gusting mountain wind, the Turkish ladies armed themselves with poles and descended upon the mob, driving them away. Just behind them came many of their husbands with pistols, sending the wild mob into hiding.

But where would the new believers go? The mob had utterly destroyed three of their houses and attacked a fourth. For a time their anger subsided, but there was still the very real threat they would attack again given an opportune moment. The dazed believers, frightened for their lives, wandered through the Turkish part of town looking for refuge from their own countrymen.

Word of the mob and the new believers spread quickly. Did these men refuse to pray to pictures? Did someone say they had a copy of the *Injil* and were trying to follow the Holy Book? Word skipped into the Turkish section, flew down the narrow streets and around the busy corners, reaching a sober-looking Turkish man standing beneath the wooden doorframe of his coffeehouse. He puffed on a cigarette then threw it to the ground. Something stirred inside him, a spark of curiosity … compassion, maybe. He could do something.

Hassan caught the attention of a beggar boy on the street and gave him instructions: go, find the homeless Armenians and bring them to his inn. The boy sped away as fast as his young legs could carry him. The Turkish streets carried the man's message into the shadows and to the refugees. Warily they stepped out of the alley feeling exhausted but extremely thankful. They made their way down the streets conscious of the silent stares of the Turkish merchants and coffee-sippers. They came to the two-storied building made of timber, plaster and stone. The Turkish owner operated a modest coffeehouse on the ground level and some guest rooms on the second floor. This would become their home for the next few weeks. The owner met them at the door. He looked serious but a friendly smile passed briefly on his sun-wrinkled face. He greeted them and turned to guide them into his humble abode, then paused for a moment and said, "Oh yes, my name is Hassan."

Some days later Cyrus Hamlin visited the refugees in Adapazari. He first went to the Turkish section and quickly wound his way through the narrow streets to find Hassan's inn. The Turkish host welcomed the tall, thin foreigner and served him a cup of coffee. The Armenian refugees met with him to discuss their situation and express their gratitude toward Hassan for giving them a safe place to stay. They felt deeply indebted to him for his gracious Anatolian hospitality. They made plans for Hamlin to go under the cover of night to visit a group of more Armenian believers who had come down from Izmit. Steppan would likewise join them. The small group of believers in Hassan's inn prayed together for God's help and for the meeting that evening.

The pre-electric villages and towns quickly darkened into inky blackness with the setting of the sun. Turkish sentries scattered throughout the town kept watch for any problems, but few people left their homes and most retired early. Hamlin quietly made his way to the boundary between the Turkish and Armenian parts and joined a group of more than twenty new believers secretly meeting in an Armenian home. Among them he found Steppan who soberly explained that the entire Armenian community in Adapazari knew of his presence and was planning an attack. They agreed he should leave town as soon as possible.

News of the planned attack reached Hassan's ears. According to Anatolian culture, he had to protect his guest at all costs. So he prepared horses and a small guard for Hamlin and himself. Hassan took his guest aside and explained. "We will rise and leave at three. A mob is planning to attack you and do you harm. The guards and myself will escort you through the city so they will do you no harm. They know better than to strike you or us lest it bring a greater problem down on their own heads. So rest now for a little."

By three the sky had begun to brighten with the slightest hint of an approaching sunrise, yet the stars could still be plainly seen. Suddenly a terrible realization came to Hamlin as he rested in his bed. In the streets just below Hassan's inn a crowd of dozens, maybe hundreds had gathered, armed with farm implements of all kinds: shovels, spades, hoes, anything to threaten, perhaps even kill the foreign missionary. He dressed and hurried down to join Hassan and the six Turkish guards in the courtyard. Though hopelessly outnumbered by the hostile mob, the six Turkish guards presented an intimidating front. Each was well over six feet tall with hardened muscles and armed from head to toe with pistols and knives. Hassan himself held a stout club in his right hand.

Together the men mounted their horses with the Turks completely surrounding their foreign guest in order to safely see him through the sea of angry people waiting outside. Hassan raised his voice and shouted to one of his servants, "Open the gate!" The group of horses waded into the crowd while Hassan yelled for people to move aside. As far as they could see in the early morning light, the faces of the men in the mob showed an evil intent. They might lash out at any moment. But the presence of the Turkish guard and the potential of arousing retribution from their Turkish neighbors kept the mob at bay.

Hamlin and Hassan slowly worked through the crowd while men begrudgingly moved aside before the great horses and their

Turkish riders. Suddenly, someone spat upon the ground in front of Hamlin's horse. Others followed with spitting, dishonoring him in clearest terms. The Turkish guards answered with cursing and threatened to strike, but he urged them to hold their peace, lest the slightest reaction ignite a deadly clash. The story continues,

> At length, we cleared the multitude, and I breathed freely. The sweet pure breath of the early morning seemed like a special gift of God. I turned to Hassan, and said. "You have saved my life; may God save yours if in danger!"

> "Koozoom. (my lamb)," he replied, "you don't understand these dogs. They are lying in wait for you behind these hedges; and I shall go with you to the river." The natural hedges along the way, thick and entangled, afforded every opportunity; but we saw nobody. When we reached the river, he said to me, "Now you have an open plain and your horse is enough for safety. I give you into God's keeping!"—a common but beautiful form of leave-taking—and so we parted.[4]

Before parting ways once outside the city, he offered Hassan a gift for his assistance in a very dangerous situation. "No, of course not," Hassan protested, holding his hand up. This perplexed Hamlin and he later reflected, "The truth is, I was his guest. I had eaten with him. He had undertaken the protection of the persecuted, and, in his mind, it was a work of piety and hospitality. I afterwards sent him a present, which he joyfully received; and I repeatedly remembered him, to his great delight. The duties of hospitality are among the most sacred of the oriental world."[5]

The years passed after that tense and difficult time, gradually easing hostilities created by the Great Anathema. The Armenian evangelical church matured and persevered with good character and peaceful intentions, even earning the respect of the community so that they could freely build a worship center in the Armenian quarter of Adapazari. Years later Hamlin decided to visit his Armenian friends there. He also had one special task in the Turkish neighborhood ... find his old friend and protector Hassan. In search of Hassan, he set out down the old familiar streets where they had faced an enraged mob. When they met again they easily recognized one another, though both had visibly aged. They embraced and talked together happily, remembering their adventure of escaping in the middle of the night. After a several moments, Hamlin reached in his pack, felt around and brought out a small gift. Hassan looked at the gift and said, "What is this?"

He responded, "After all these years and for the rest of my life I'm sure I will never forget all you have done for me. My friends will never forget either. One of them, a close friend from New York, sent you this gift. I'm presenting it on his behalf. Please take it, you must really." Hamlin later said Hassan was, "profoundly surprised and delighted ... however, it was inexplicable to him that a distant stranger should either know or care for what he regarded as a mere act of hospitality."[6]

Hassan lived a hundred and fifty years ago in Adapazari, Turkey. Did he have children, grandchildren? Do his descendants still live there? Did they perhaps migrate along with millions of other villagers into the ever-growing municipalities of Istanbul? The terrified Armenians who discovered a safe haven in Hassan's inn were not Muslims. From the point of view of their own countrymen, they were not good Christians either. They had come under the *anathema* for their decision to read the Bible and think for themselves. When others despised and threatened them, Hassan, a Turkish Muslim, offered them honor and helped save their lives. One person offers protection for people who believe differently … another threatens to kill them. Why such vastly different reactions?

When Life and Honor are Threatened

In the 1850s the Ottoman sultan tried to strengthen religious freedom in the empire with a decree called the *Hatti-Sherif*. One of its articles granted people the right to defend themselves from persecution. It declared, "What man, whatever may be his detestation of violence, would refrain from having recourse to it, and thereby injuring the government and his country, if his life and honor are exposed to danger?"

Fast forward fifty years from the world of the sultan and Hassan. The Ottoman and other European empires ended with the dawn of a new century. The Russian Czar fell to the Communists, the British Empire faded and French and German colonies became independent. Interethnic relationships between the Muslim Turks and Armenian Christians, both Orthodox and

Evangelical, deteriorated into some of the worst violence of the 20th century. The scorched-earth policy of the Turks resulted in the deaths of hundreds of thousands of men, women and children, nearly pushing the ancient Christian peoples completely out of Anatolia. Using any means possible and sometimes in spite of no co-operation from Western governments, some of these persecuted people managed to catch a boat or a ship to a friendly port. Evangelical Armenians arrived in America optimistic that their churches could flourish under a free and democratic government.

In 1922 Istanbul saw the end of the Caliphate and the rise of secular Turkey. "No nation was ever founded with greater revolutionary zeal than the Turkish Republic," writes Stephen Kinzer, "nor has any undergone more sweeping change in such a short time."[7] Turkey's founder, Kemal Mustafa Atatürk, introduced new clothing, a new alphabet, new laws, a new Islam, new values and new philosophies.

Ending Islamic *Sharia* law, Atatürk hoped for a new era of enlightenment (*laiklik*), brought about by education and European secular law. He believed the industrious and intelligent Turkish nation could take its place among the leaders of the earth if it was just given a chance to modernize. Islam would continue to play a role in the lives of Turks, but in a different way. Atatürk "banned mystic religious sects, forbade the wearing of religious garb and denounced superstitions dwelling in people's minds. In an assault on religious authority comparable to Luther's, he ordered the Koran translated into Turkish so the ordinary people could read it for themselves rather than relying on the interpretations of Islamic teachers."[8]

After Atatürk's death, Turkish politicians and academics have continued to develop his vision of a modern Islam. They created a curious blend of nationalistic fervor, secular lifestyle and religious fear that has effectively isolated Turkey from the rest of the Islamic world and undermined its relationships with the West. One popular Turkish author, Yaşar Nuri Öztürk, made an Atatürk-friendly Turkish translation of the Qur'an and wrote a number of books reinterpreting Islam. A sentry for Turkish Islam, he warns that the United States government is working with conservative Muslims to re-establish the Islamic Caliphate across the Middle East. Pointing to a US foreign policy called the *Greater Middle Eastern Project*, conspiracy theorists like Öztürk believe the US will use the new Islamic Caliphate as a puppet government through which they can dominate and exploit the Muslim world.[9]

Many Muslims in Turkey and beyond share Öztürk's fears. They fear Western (which they translate Christendom) dominance and forced conversion to Christianity. Turkish religious leader Fikret Karaman from Elazığ published a formal essay called, "The Activity of Missionaries Yesterday and Today." Like Öztürk, he feels threatened by Christians. He writes, "In every time of history, religions, philosophies and ideologies have desired to pull ahead in a competition with one another." Karaman cites Matthew 28:18–20 to explain the source of Christianity's impulse to globalize, but then he makes an odd leap of logic and says, "this is the source of Christian mission, but it doesn't stop there. Many times it has been combined with activities of military, economic and cultural exploitation." He adds, "Their essential goal is Western hegemony, through preparing a spiritual foundation ... sometimes the missionaries come as soldiers, sometimes as doctors, sometimes teachers and sometimes Peace Corps volunteers." In contrast to the threat of Christian missions, Karaman asserted, "Islam provides the solutions for a person's world and unchanging happiness, his peace and well-being and everything good. Historically Islam has never used coercive propaganda or force to make any group or minority accept it."

Intensifying their anti-Christian conspiracy theories in the late 20th and early 21st centuries, national and local media in Turkey took up the subject of missionary work, running countless articles and programs. Press articles conveyed the impression that the US, Israel and the EU sponsored missionary activity for political purposes. One said, "They especially like to prey upon ethnic differences, differences in religious sects, economic and political difficulties and even destructive disasters like earthquakes and floods to proselytize our children and youth ... " The article continued, "Savor this fact ... every day in the churches they pray, 'Apart from Jesus there is no salvation' ... Their purpose is not religious communication, but political.'" The day after the Malatya murders, a top-level Turkish official named Niyazi Guney expressed his opinion to the national press. "Missionary activity in Turkey is going on uncontrolled like it was during the last era of the Ottoman Empire ... missionary activity is more dangerous than a terror organization and unfortunately, it isn't considered a crime."

Peeling the Onion

Social networks can be compared to an onion. An onion has many layers, it can produce delicious seasoning and it can bring tears to the eye. Furthermore, not all onions are the same.

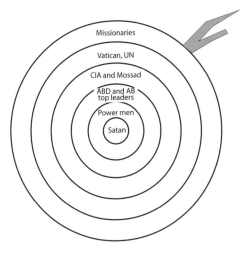

While one onion may have gone rotten or become poisonous, another might be perfectly sound and healthy. Many Turkish journalists, writers, religious leaders, military and police officers and politicians have studied the history of the so-called "Christian" West and come to the conclusion that the Christian faith, culture, politics and economics are inseparable. Perhaps some of them judge Christianity through their own lens of the Islamic Caliphate, where *Sharia* law governed both civil and spiritual matters. Many Muslims form their opinions about Christianity by watching how countries have sponsored state churches in the past. Catholic, Orthodox and Protestant churches have at times taken an active role in temporal politics. Italy is predominantly Catholic, England predominantly Anglican and Russia still predominately Russian Orthodox, even atheistic Communism worked hard for seventy years to destroy all religions. Many Muslims pick up the Christian onion like the first illustration and start peeling off layers, quickly concluding that there is an alliance between Western governments and their churches to drive Muslims out of Turkey and reclaim the ancient land.

Mehmet Peels the Onion

One sunny spring afternoon in Istanbul a young man named

Mehmet returned home from a job interview. Walking down a wide boulevard, weaving in and out of traffic and pedestrians, he met a friendly person who offered him a booklet explaining some of the basic beliefs of Christians. On the back of the booklet he found a website address with more information. After glancing through the booklet he tossed it to the ground in disgust. In his worldview, the booklet was just the first layer of a rotten onion. He mentally peeled the onion, layer after layer. The first layer was a harmless looking booklet with a couple of nice photographs and a few verses taken from the *Injil*. But who handed it to him? He didn't look very closely, so he couldn't remember if it was a foreigner or a Turk, though it really didn't matter to him, because they were just the second layer of the onion. He imagined that behind them was a missionary organization. And what is behind the missionary organization? He peeled another layer off the imaginary onion, guessing that the CIA or some other dark organization was behind the missionary organization. And behind that layer? He peeled off another layer in his mind. Yes, behind them was a plan of intrigue carried on by "Crusader" powers of the West, bent on undermining his country and religion. He believed

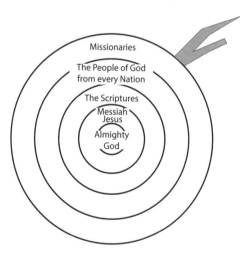

Aim: Proclaim the Good News of Jesus to all peoples, tribes, and languages so each individual can see for himself or herself.

they had been making trouble in his homeland since the days of the Ottoman Empire.

But he suspected an even more sinister layer at work.

He paused for a moment wondering, maybe some very secretive and dark forces were at work in high places. Beyond them could only be Satan. Mehmet concluded the onion was rotten at best and poisonous at worse, posing a dire threat to his honor and his life. And though Mehmet was not a violent man, he could be aroused to defend his life and honor if threatened.

But was he peeling the right onion? What if Mehmet had looked at the little booklet with a different set of presuppositions? Perhaps he feels a little suspicious, but being an intelligent person, refuses to jump to conclusions without a fair evaluation. So he pockets the booklet until he can get home to his computer. At home he browses a website from the back cover that presents information about the Bible. Some of it contradicts things he has been taught. Wasn't the Bible changed? Didn't God take Jesus to heaven before he died on the cross? What about missionaries? At home Mehmet visits a website with information about missionaries and peels another layer off the onion. Behind the missionaries he discovers churches from a variety of nations and lands on every continent. He removes another layer. Who is behind the churches? The CIA, the Mossad, other shadowy organizations? No, they claim to look to the *Tevrat, Zebur,* and *Injil* as their source of inspiration and authority. But what about the Holy Book, is it trustworthy? He peels off another layer. The Bible that existed in Muhammad's day was the same as the one that existed 500 years earlier. Mehmet studies the onion in his hand, considering for the first time in his life that the Christian onion might actually be sound and healthy in every layer down to the core.

The Voice of a Church Leader

How do Turkish church leaders feel about these suspicions they live with every day? One church leader named Dogan shared his thoughts about the problems.

Is it true that a Turkish citizen who becomes a Christian commits an act of treason? Dogan thinks, "absolutely not. I can say for myself, after coming to Jesus Christ, I could love my people and country. Necati and Uğur were men who loved their people and lived among their own people sharing the love of Jesus and the good news of salvation. It may be hard to live among our people as a Christian but the motivation and wish that directed these men was the love of Jesus Christ."

But what if there is a war, whose side will the believer take? Dogan responds, "This also is one example from many comical ideas, because these ideas come from not knowing what's in the Injil. Romans chapter 13 clearly says that Christians must live under the authority which they find themselves. I am a citizen of Turkey so I'm tied to the Republic of Turkey. The prime ministry of the land is my prime minister. The president of Turkey is my president. I pray for them because the Holy Book says we should especially pray for our leaders. I pray for them and for my people. The Injil instructs me to keep the laws of the land. If there is a war, I will do what I can to support the people on my own side. The idea of treason is ridiculous and impossible for someone like Necati who kept God's Word."

Are Christians on a mission to tear apart the fabric of the country? "In my opinion," says Dogan, "when a person of another belief encounters a different belief with insufficient understanding, there is a desire to view the person with a different belief as an enemy. I'm sorry to say, without having sufficient information about the different belief, people can create a kind of panic by focusing on ideas about destroying the country, creating disunity, and sparking provocations."

Thinking about the nature of God's Kingdom, he continues, "Before Jesus hung on the cross, the ruler in Jerusalem Pontius Pilate asked Jesus, 'Are you a king?' Jesus answered, 'My kingdom is not from this world.' I mean that Jesus' dominion and kingdom is not like the things from this world we understand, it's not a political thing or related to anything political. God's dominion is in a person's heart where everything is submitted to him first of all. Such a person doesn't lie, doesn't pay bribes and doesn't speak evil of his neighbor, I wish for many more such people in Turkey."

But how can the church respond to the widespread fear that Christianity is a tool of Western Imperialism? "There's nothing remotely close to politics in Scripture and Christianity. The Injil gives no commands for such a thing and Jesus never entered politics, it has nothing to do with Christianity."

On April 18, 2007 news outlets around the world broadcast the news that a group of five young Turkish men entered the offices of three missionaries and brutally murdered them. For years before this act of destruction, the Turkish media, government and academia have continuously repeated this message: missionaries are an internal threat to honor and life. They created the myth of the first onion. Their message repeated endlessly on the radio, television, internet, in newspapers and from government offices has sunk down into the worldview of the nation. The first kind of onion with its rottenness and poison has been lifted up as an example for all to see. It has never entered the mind of many that the second healthy onion might exist. Many others refuse to entertain the idea that it ever could.

10 Road to Malatya

Tilmann and Susanne arrived in Malatya during a rain storm, feeling less than inspired by the gray skies and bleak skyline. The inclement weather left a bad impression that called for a second chance, so they decided to make another visit to Malatya in the spring, taking along their children. When they arrived in May, the beauty of Malatya's green hills and orchards thrilled their kids. They definitely liked the place better than the cement and dust of Adana. So the Geskes set out to find a home to rent. To their amazement and delight, they found a new apartment that fit their limited budget, for just 150 lira a month, equivalent to about 100 dollars. For a down payment they offered the landlord all they had in their pocket, just 20 lira. He took it, sealing their future in Malatya.

In 2003 the Geskes moved to Malatya, Tilmann proceeded to set up his consulting business and they began making friends. However, the arrival of a Turkish-speaking German family in an eastern Turkish city like Malatya, where there were few other foreigners, brought a severe reaction. Television stations and newspapers began discussing their arrival, stirring suspicion, fear and animosity. They sought to sniff out and implicate the new residents with a darker agenda than simply wishing to make Turkish friends and share their personal faith in Jesus. Following the trend of many national news articles and official statements, the local Malatya press sought to accuse the believers of secretly working to destroy the values of the youth, bring dishonor upon the community and undermine the Turkish state.

Tilmann had been fully aware that such suspicions might arise with his arrival. He wrote a letter to his friends in Germany, "For a Turkish man or woman, what could be as horrible as a Christian missionary? They think a missionary is someone who wants to tear apart the land, or is a spy for the EU, a preacher of Jesus, a brainwasher, and an activist for the Kurds."

A Turkish believer later expressed deep sorrow for how Tilmann suffered saying, "For Tilmann, coming as a foreign German, it was a hard thing to leave his own culture, people and language for our culture and live among us. His children had to learn to live among a people they didn't know and learn a new language and culture. That such a thing as this would happen to him is really unthinkable for Turks because our people normally place such a high value on hospitable treatment of guests, especially one that has come like Tilmann with no bad or ulterior motives. Like Necati, Tilmann wanted to share with others the love of the Messiah."

Tilmann and Susanne talked much and prayed often during the period of intense media persecution. In a way it seemed almost comical, that their humble family was being treated like some sort of celebrity or worse. After all, in reality he was no spy or agent of a foreign government. Back in Germany the most dangerous job he ever had was driving a forklift in a warehouse. He hadn't come to Turkey to debate, argue or insult. He wrote his friends back home, "What are some of the effective ways of introducing people to Jesus? It is good for people to hear about Jesus through friendly meetings and getting his message out far and wide. Others even have had dreams where they have seen Jesus visit them personally." Living in Adana and then Malatya, Tilmann and his family showed their respect for the Republic by obeying its laws, paying necessary taxes and honoring its officials. The bizarre caricature the press had created of him was completely disconnected from his real identity and purposes. He and Susanne prayed often hoping that people would someday see the truth and discover who they really were: not a threat, just genuinely concerned friends.

Trying to ignore the false reports as best he could, Tilmann patiently continued to work with integrity, loving his family and building relationships with his Turkish friends, believing that in time he would see fruit for his labor. With his superior language skills, Tilmann grew his business called Silk Road Consultancy. His Turkish proficiency improved to a high level of fluency, eventually earning him formal certification in Germany as a Turkish-German translator.

The natural beauty around Malatya often coaxed Tilmann out to the countryside. He loved to take his bicycle on long treks across the steppe, enjoying the soaring vistas and the mosaics of apricot orchards. He shared his love for nature and sports with his children, teaching them to play soccer, basketball and other sports. He had been a champion rower in younger days and loved following Formula I racing. The kids admired their tall, athletic father who, though quiet and reserved, had a strong competitive streak and always seemed to win in the end.

For Necati, several trips to Kutahya, porcelain capital of Turkey, had confirmed his desire to move eastward. There were already several Turkish churches in Izmir, but the vast interior of Anatolia had countless cities, towns and villages where no one had ever seen a copy of the Bible, much less read it. Necati had a shepherd's heart to go out in search of the lost sheep. Trips to Kutahya gave the Aydins a new hope and joy in taking the good news of Jesus to others who had never heard.

Chatting one day over tea a friend mentioned the city of Malatya to Necati. The name intrigued him ... Malatya ... deep in the heart of Turkey, the center of the world's apricot production, a city with long history and intense national pride. Other believers were moving there as well, some foreigners. He didn't feel uncomfortable with foreigners since he knew that in the Messiah all nationalities could be one. He and Shemse decided to pray and talk more about Malatya. Is this where God was calling them? Orhan and his wife joined their friends in prayer and planning. They eventually came to have a settled assurance and peace in their hearts. Yes, the Aydins would move to Malatya, though Orhan's family would stay in Izmir.

One supervisor later commented, "I think he just loved Jesus. You know, he loved people. And he wanted them to find the hope that he had. And he was totally humble. I mean, I never heard him speak poorly of anyone, I never heard him say anything like a complaint about his time in jail or any of the difficulties they faced. He was working in our Izmir office and knew that we wanted to get an office further east in the country. You know, that's a hard move for anybody. He came up to me and volunteered and said, 'You know, Shemse and I think this is something we are ready to do. And we want to do this.' So it was through that and through a group of other believers, Tilmann being one of them, that they ended up working together on the church and we were able to open our office out there, so it was very cool."

Moving to Malatya meant lots of fresh apricots, green hillsides for the children to enjoy, uninvited attention from the press and the beginning of a new friendship between Necati and Tilmann. In natural terms, the two men had many differences and few things in common. One had come from northern Europe, the other born in Erzurum. One from a people nominally Christian, the other from a pious Muslim family. One, tall, lanky, blond and fair, the other short, swarthy, dark and strikingly handsome. But where their natural similarities ended, their spiritual compatibility started. Both men had settled into Malatya with their wives and small children, committing to live in the Turkish heartland serving the Turkish people in spite of being misunderstood, defamed, defrauded … or much worse. They both felt that God had very clearly called them, one from Adana and one from Izmir, to live in Malatya as salt and light.

When Tilmann and Necati met, they could each sense in the other a deep seriousness and maturity, almost beyond their years. Necati respected Tilmann's obvious language abilities and that he had given himself to mastering the Turkish language as a bridge to speak meaningfully to Turkish friends. Tilmann appreciated Necati's ability to remain joyful and hopeful in the midst of obvious hardships like rejection from family and friends, hostility from fellow countrymen and human rights abuses. A cross-cultural friendship began between the two men that would carry them until the very end.

Likewise their two families would become closely related while living together in Malatya. They met regularly to enjoy meals, celebrate birthdays, play games, pray and worship together. In a way, the Geskes and Aydins became family. Language was really no problem since the Geskes had become thoroughly at home in Turkey. Their children went to Turkish school and spoke Turkish like second nature. In the mid-2000s they enjoyed many sweet days of friendship, happily sharing their joys and concerns knowing that the other would listen and do anything he could to help.

The small group of Christians in Malatya had a deep commitment to prayer. They regularly talked to God, asking his involvement and help for each other and for their neighbors. Prayer for them was not limited to a certain time or place. They prayed anywhere, anytime. On one occasion some of them gathered in the center of Malatya to pray for the prosperity of the city, asking God to bless the inhabitants with his love, grace and abundant life found in Jesus the Messiah. Standing on the sidewalk with Tilmann and some others, Susanne watched the

bustling crowds of young and old people. Her heart was moved
with compassion as she looked upon the masses. What would
it take for them to understand how much God loves them? As
the group of three or four stood quietly asking God to bless
Malatya and Turkey, a word came to Susanne, as though God was
answering her question, "It will take the shedding of blood for the
people to understand how much God loves them."

In the first few years in Malatya, Necati conducted Zirve
business from an office in the commercial district, but some
problems came up with the facilities requiring him to relocate.
One day he approached Tilmann to make an offer. "Tilmann,"
he said, "Maybe you heard that my company Zirve needs to find
some new office space."

"Has there been trouble?"

"Well, nothing major, but I think we need a different place to
set up our business. And I was wondering if you would like to
share the space with us. You could have your own room. My new
partner Uğur and I would take the main room."

"Yes, I think that would be fine. Let me talk with Susanne and I
will get back to you."

"Thank you. Let me know when you make a decision. We
would be happy for you to be nearby."

Some days later Tilmann spoke with Necati. "About that office
space …"

"Yes, so you make a decision?" Necati responded hopefully. "Like I said, we would be happy to have you nearby."

"I think that could be a good arrangement. Let me know what I need to do to get moved in."

Necati smiled, "Yes, of course brother Tilmann. Thank you!"

One of the men Necati had come to know quite well during his visits throughout the region was Uğur Yuksel. In spite of having suffered with the hardship of losing his cell phone business in Elazığ, Uğur had kept his faith in the Lord. He and Necati became best of friends and over the months Necati taught and equipped Uğur to grow in his faith and share it with others. Uğur impressed Necati with his humble attitude and eagerness to learn. He impressed him so much in his character that Necati decided to approach his supervisor and request that Zirve hire Uğur as a partner in Malatya. It made good sense. Uğur and Necati had a good friendship, Uğur was from Elazığ, just an hour to the east of Malatya, he came from an Alevi background whereas Necati had been a Sunni and so they complimented one another in their ability to speak meaningfully to different kinds of people.

Zirve leadership fully trusted Necati, who at that time had been promoted to regional leadership, so they hired Uğur to begin work in Malatya. Uğur became well acquainted with the small but growing group of believers in Malatya, including Tilmann, who shared the Zirve office. Uğur, a bit of a comic, would often entertain the two more serious and quiet men with his jokes and antics. He never lacked a cheerful smile or another silly facial expression.

Yet the suspicions remained high. People couldn't understand why a Turk could identify with the Messiah Jesus. With insight a Turkish believer later talked about their motivation for becoming Christians. These seemed like educated men, intelligent, thoughtful. Were they crazy or brain-washed or deceived, or paid money? "The basic motivation is that in a person's heart, he is truly motivated with the desire to search for God and find Jesus Christ, I mean Necati, Uğur and other people in Turkey who have identified with Christianity researched whether or not it is true. They wanted to know if the *Injil* was changed or not, whether Jesus really died on the cross or not, so they looked into the truth. Essentially, they saw this eye-catching billboard: these falsehoods and accusations of the last centuries, about the Bible being changed are simply not possible, because the *Injil* is God's Word and Jesus himself said that heaven and earth would pass away but his word would never pass away. So Jesus Christ's words have not passed away and his words are in the Injil unchanged and unchangeable. I knew these men personally and they weren't deceived, for that matter Necati was an honest person to the highest degree."

During 2005 and 2006 Necati and Uğur stayed constantly busy providing material for sale at book fairs, visiting persons curious to study more and taking turns teaching the small group of believers in the city. Tilmann worked hard teaching English, providing translation and consulting services, caring for his family and in his free time helping with the small church. The men and their families enjoyed one another as their friendships deepened during times spent around the Turkish *mangal* (barbecue) making shish kebobs, sharing a tea in the office or praying for one another in their homes.

In 2006 Necati's relationship with his extended family had become so strained he felt he could do nothing else but ask them to cease communication. The pressure and criticism about his faith had continued unabated. After much intense soul-searching, he wrote a personal letter to his family explaining his faith in Jesus and his desire to live in peace with them as much as was possible from his side. After his death, newspapers across Turkey made his personal and heartfelt letter famous.

Dear Mother and Father, brother and sisters,

First of all, I want to greet and kiss you in the glorious name of the Lord Jesus Christ. After dozens of time we've had confusion and conflicts, in order to protect my firm decision to trust in the Messiah Jesus as I live to the end, I want to protect this truth, so I have made the decision to separate myself from you.

I'm not making this decision out of fear or any wish or desire that I have about anything, it's a decision I've come to after a long period of debating within myself and going back and forth. So please don't blame anyone or try to speculate in vain about this decision. I've returned to the place I belong, to Jesus and to those he has gathered to himself. I have a spiritual family now just as I have you as a physical family. Please don't worry or fret because of my separating myself from you. Because I'm not in a situation of loss, to the contrary, I've been saved and have gained eternal life. I mean, you at last have a child who has been saved. Rejoice for this reason.

I've won this salvation through my faith in Jesus and nothing, no deprivation, no hardship, no sickness, no evil, no death and no person has the power to turn me away from his salvation.

With all my strength and the life in my veins I am tied with Jesus through the way of faith. His life, death and current absence mean for us the right of eternal life. From this time on, I will be related to you as a son and a brother and I will be in a constant state of prayer for you ... for your salvation. For now, I don't want you to contact me by telephone or any way. However, I want time to pass with you patiently waiting, so that the hate in your hearts will be erased and replaced by love and compassion and I wish for your understanding to be knitted in such a way that as you get to know the most important One, the 'truth, way and life', Jesus Messiah, you will put your faith in him earning eternal life. I love you. May God answer you with the truth. Amen.

Rana Necati Aydin

 # Making
a Name

Night and day Necati's work took him to distant towns and villages. Sometimes he followed crude roads where a gaping pothole would be a welcome change from having to dodge land mines. The small group of believers in Malatya offered support and friendship to his family while he spent time away. His dynamic work ethos, thorough understanding of the Qur'an and the *Tevrat, Zebur* and *Injil*, combined with his warm, personal faith in Jesus the Messiah, distinguished him as an effective evangelist who quickly brought people into the fledgling church. Even though public criticisms and outright lies about Christianity continued unabated throughout his ministry, Necati kept a good attitude, optimistically focusing on the fact that while many disbelieved, some had understood and accepted the message of salvation in Jesus. The men reminded themselves that

Jesus himself had said his followers would face hardships but that he had already overcome it all.

In addition to doing evangelism, Necati drew upon considerable spiritual and cultural insight when equipping other believers to express their faith in Turkey. He explained that the core of the Gospel rests on four basic truths: humans have sinned and are separated from God, people try to overcome the sin and separation through good works but fail in their efforts, according to God's own plan he sent Jesus Christ to take the punishment for humanity's sin, those who trust in Jesus are saved by grace. In one training module he wrote in more detail,

The Vision of Evangelism:

To faithfully build a bridge between lost humanity and Christ the Savior.

Before going out to tell others the Good News:

We aren't in this work to build our own dominions or win praise for ourselves, but to serve the Lord for his glory. Prayer moves the hand of God. We need to go out with the proper training and equipping. We need to go out with a clean heart, and mind, anointed by the Holy Spirit and with a clean conscience.

Meet people in appropriate contexts:

It's important to find the right time and place for talking to people. We must keep ourselves and our work unstained.

Above all, love and understanding:

As we listen to people with sensitivity, we hear their hardships and weaknesses with understanding, sometimes we smile and sometimes we cry.

We need to share our lives with others:

If we approach people as if we are a kind of hunter, our relationship with them will be limited and short. But as we enter their special life circumstances, we can win a trusting relationship. Even by participating in weddings, celebrations and ceremonies. Sometimes we can strengthen our relationships as we talk about our own lives, our families, our past life experiences and our inner life.

Approach people as friends, not strangers

The person we are speaking with may have a different lifestyle or different traditions, but we should try to relate to them. In some village homes, not sitting on their floor pads or not drinking ayran and eating tandir bread will make them feel very strange. If we can't accept their culture, how can we expect to convince them to accept our God? Instead of coming like some creature from outer space, we need to come as our Lord did possessing humility.

They should become a better child and citizen.

We don't give any false hope of money or a future:

In our country, a widespread perception is that Christians give out money, property and work. In addition to our words, we prove with a humble and modest lifestyle that our freedom and blessings brought about in Christ don't come from material wealth.

Directing people to holiness and the truth:

Our first goal of our ministry is to explain the holiness of God, and we present the solution to sin. sharing the teaching about discipline found in God's word.

Sharing the truths and gifts of the Holy Spirit:

Opening minds blinded by sin and purifying thoughts is a work only done by the Holy Spirit. To move in the Holy Spirit in our witnessing we need to be controlled by the Spirit, sharing his gifts.

Showing respect in the discussion of values: We need to express respect for the values and customs of other people.

Empty talk and argumentation:

We need to avoid debates with people of other religions and ideas. If we don't, it will push us away from our goal, which is to offer a peaceful conversation.

One of Necati's concerns was that people see practical ways that God loves them. Many passages in the Bible motivated him to think of creative ways to serve the community and the poor. One day he had the idea to serve a village where the public school needed a facelift. Necati organized a work project with several volunteers who spent their vacation time during two consecutive summers repairing the school. Afterwards, Necati wrote a report about the village project.

Our second summer "School Restoration Project" took a much more interesting course than last year's. Months before we started the project, planned for the beginning of June, we did some research into the primary school of a village that we had chosen. We took notes about their needs and finally started working with all the necessary permissions. Twenty university students from another country took part in the project. All the guest students stayed in the village with local families in ten different houses. This gave them the opportunity of both sharing the gospel and learning quite a lot about village culture.

In one of the houses where they stayed lived a young girl who was a believer. Their presence as brothers and sisters in Christ greatly encouraged her and gave her joy. During daytime the students worked very hard renovating the school and as believers in Christ, they were good witnesses to the youths of the village who kept coming to talk with them. When the students returned to the houses in the evenings, they were both a source of joy to the families and had the opportunity for sharing the gospel. All the people of the village knew that we were Christians. That's why they thought and talked more about this subject. Yet some of the villagers who felt uncomfortable tried to hinder us by complaining to the police, saying we were doing missionary work. Despite all their attempts we stayed there until the work was finished and we maintained a good witness. The majority of villagers were very happy about us being there and greatly approved of what we had done. During the whole time until the project was finished we shared the Gospel with several people. The fact that the villagers opened their houses and hearts to us and the opportunity of sharing the gospel with quite a number of people in different ways was a very important and interesting experience.

Necati had a shepherd's heart and his flock needed not only physical bread and drink but spiritual nourishment. Along with Tilmann he carried in his heart the burden of watching over the members of the small Malatya church. He wanted people not just to hear information about Jesus; he wanted them to grow in their relationship with him, becoming spiritually mature. In September 2006 Necati penned this short note to his friends, saying,

The house group in Malatya is growing, with 15 people confessing faith. Since some of these are youth who are dealing with negative reactions and problems in their homes, we are trying to support them ... By God's grace we're talking to more people every day.

After working with us for three years, some South African friends were unable to extend their residence permits, so they must return to their country. A church in Ankara is sending a young couple to come join us in their place.

In response to the problems and needs, we are sharing the faith with more enthusiasm. The house fellowship in Malatya and neighboring cities is continuing to be a light.

By this time hostile articles in the local press had diminished, but in March 2006 Tilmann encountered problems renewing his work permit, so he wrote a letter to the Ministry of Labor appealing his position. He also wrote to the Malatya regional government requesting their assistance saying, "We are a family who has settled in Turkey and who loves this country. Our three children (aged 1, 4 and 6) have had all their school experience in Turkey. For this reason, we request that you extend our residence permits to June so we don't have to go out of the country from Malatya." The problem was resolved after some weeks, but not without much stress and effort on Tilmann's behalf to keep his family living quietly and respectfully in Malatya.

The small church in Malatya continued meeting weekly to study the Bible, worship the Lord, pray and enjoy fellowship with one another. At special times they celebrated significant events in the life of Jesus. In December 2006 the group made plans for a large Christmas outreach. They rented a conference room in a local hotel and worked together planning the program with a festival of music and presentations. The successful Christmas outreach encouraged them to plan another one the following Easter.

Weeks before Easter Necati and Uğur joined some believers in another city for rest and encouragement. During one worship period something unusual happened. One of the men in attendance recalled it saying, "At our last meeting together about one month before the murders, we met in a hotel. Necati asked the group, 'Who would give his life for his brother? Who would be willing to lay down his life for his brother serving with him in ministry? Would you be willing to lay down your life for your brother?' One of the brothers answered, it was Uğur, Necati's ministry partner, 'I would give my life without hesitation. I would give my life for the Lord Jesus and I would give my life for my brother.' That really impacted me. And they had been threatened, especially in Malatya where there are many religious and nationalistic groups, where it's a really difficult city, not at all an easy place, they tried to frighten them. But Necati and Uğur both said, 'We're not afraid, we're staying, we're doing the Lord's work.' Necati's words have never left me and I asked myself if I would give my life for my brother, could I abandon my life?"

Another brother at the same meeting put it this way, "In our last meeting he raised the question, who would give their life for their friend. But sadly, because everyone was involved in their own problems, we didn't give the right answer; we didn't say we would give our lives for our friends. The only one who answered was Uğur. He said he would give his life for his friends. No one else answered. We will be judged for that because we didn't put value on our brother to the point of willingness to die for him. It was just a simple question Necati asked. He said told how Jesus said that there is no greater love than this, that a person would lay down his life for his friend. Do you know what Necati's one expectation was for all the teams he managed? He wrote a letter to every team saying, 'I'm not expecting you to give a heroic answer, but could you say that with the Lord's strength you would be willing to lay down your life for your brother.'"

That spring Uğur met with one of his mentors, a man named Farhat, who would later understand their conversation in a new light. Farhat said, "In our last meeting we shared personal concerns and I sensed something in Uğur. He had given everything for the sake of the gospel of the Messiah. I mean, in our lengthy conversation, he expressed things I don't think he was even conscious of, as though God had prepared him for the things to come. He showed great courage, saying how he would continue to work for the Messiah, as though maybe he had a feeling of something in the region he was working. I don't remember his exact words and I didn't exactly understand what he meant, but do you understand, God had strengthened him and given him great courage. What am I trying to say ... I believe that Uğur had taken up his cross and knew he could die. His father told him in his last conversation with him, 'son, they will kill you, they can kill you and will kill you. Give up this road you're on.' But Uğur had taken up his cross Necati was the same. When I looked at him I saw the most Christ-like example I knew. When I looked at Necati I saw Jesus because whenever we had problems, we waited for him to be upset or offended, but even when he had to say no, he was always positive. If he did get angry, he always smiled, showing kindness and love. He had a great influence on us. The seeds he has sown throughout the region are still bearing fruit as people remember him and his influence upon us."

Tilmann and Susanne rarely had disagreements. His quiet nature readily adapted to her energetic personality and he felt satisfied to do whatever he could to make her happy and content. This had been their communication style for almost two decades and had worked very well for both of them. They simply didn't argue and fight, their home was peaceful and they lived agreeably. That's what made their argument a few weeks after the Christmas program very strange. After years of peaceful married life, they had their first serious disagreement. Tilmann felt the time had come for them to leave Turkey. He wanted to finish some important translation and academic projects he was working on then move his family back to Germany.

Something inside him seemed to say that his time was almost done in Turkey. Susanne felt differently. She didn't want to leave and didn't feel their work was over. The discussion became heated, even loud, with their voices raised as each tried to argue their own side. This had never happened before in their relationship and it brought stress. In the end they wisely agreed to stop arguing and pray about the matter, leaving it closed until a suitable time. The suitable time never came, but circumstances two months later seemed to show they had both been right.

Necati and Shemse welcomed the believers into their living room one evening. Everyone felt weary from office work, visiting friends, tending to children, cooking and cleaning, but for these few quiet moments together, they each turned inwardly, examining their hearts. Tilmann spoke. "Before we take the Lord's Supper, we need to each search our hearts and confess our sins. The Lord is quick to forgive us, but let us not take the Lord's Supper until we make sure our relationship with the Lord is in order." He took a plate with a piece of bread upon it, broke the bread into pieces and distributed it. Then he took a cup of grape juice and handed it to each person. He read from the Bible, "This is my body, which is for you. Do this in memory of me. In the same way, after the supper he took the cup and said, 'this cup is God's new covenant, sealed with my blood. Whenever you drink it, do so in memory of me'. This means that every time you eat this bread and drink from this cup you proclaim the Lord's death until he comes." Susanne and the kids, Necati and Shemse, Uğur and others each somberly received the bread and drink, silently giving thanks for the one who died for them.

In his widespread roaming and scattering the spiritual seed

in difficult and disappointing circumstances, Necati never lost hope for a harvest. An unexpected encounter with a farmer one afternoon left him with unforgettable encouragement. Necati later wrote,

> From this area we've had opportunities to spread the word to farmers, shepherds and local people. We went north on the highway to another town. We had the opportunity to speak with an abundance of people working in the fields. We spoke to one person who said, "Your work will bear fruit someday, but it will take patience and a long time." It was like he had spoken a word from God to us, giving hope and heartening us. After that we turned back to the next region.

 # Bloodied hands

My child, when sinners tempt you, don't give in. Suppose they say, 'Come on; let's find someone to kill! Let's attack some innocent people for the fun of it! They may be alive and well when we find them, but they'll be dead when we're through with them!' (Proverbs 1:10–12)

Five young men, born in Turkey during the turbulent days of political and social transition of the 1980s, became acquainted with one another in Malatya. The men were Emre Gunaydin, Salih Gurler, Hamit Ceker, Abuzer Yildirim, and Cuma Ozdemir. A glance at the five young men revealed nothing extraordinary. Each one looked like a normal Turkish man, more or less average height, dark hair, the beginnings of black whiskers growing on their faces barely masking the softness of a boy. The

Turkish language has a word for men in their late adolescence, it is *delikanli*, meaning "crazy blood." In the instance of these five Muslim men of Malatya, the label would become lethally accurate.

One of the five, Emre Gunaydin, graduated from high school in Malatya and eventually moved into a college dormitory there. His father worked at the local Inonu University and owned a martial arts center called Kobra Kan. Somewhere along the way in 2006 Emre became interested in missionaries and missionary activity in Turkey. He knew people in various nationalistic organizations and had a girlfriend whose father was a member of a nationalistic political party. He had grown up during the years when many members of the Turkish press, educational system and government fostered deep suspicion and hostility toward Christians and missionaries, loading these terms with negative, even diabolical meanings. He and his friends saw themselves as heroes and missionaries as monsters.

According to his testimony, Emre happened to view a television program in 2006 covering the subject of missionary activity in Turkey. When reading an article or watching a program about missionary activity, a normal Turkish person might feel apathy, curiosity, fear, anger or rage. Some would likely dismiss the whole thing as an exaggeration, but a great many would feel threatened. The memory of the television program stuck in his mind, raising questions. The internet allowed him to research the matter more carefully. He began looking at Christian websites. They confirmed some of the things the programs and articles had said: some Turkish Muslims had in the last few years become Christians. Any informed Muslim knows that historically, while persons of any religious background can become a Muslim, no Muslim should be allowed to leave Islam. The street runs in one direction. Since Islam is a comprehensive social, political and religious system, at least in its ideal form, leaving it amounts to treason. Emre's internet research led him down the trail closer to his own home town of Malatya.

He eventually exchanged emails with a Turkish believer living in Izmit, the same town Mr. Steppan first met the missionaries a hundred and fifty years earlier. From that contact he got Necati's email address and wrote him a short note on March 13, 2007. Feigning interest in Christianity and using the false name Yunus Emre, he wrote Necati, "Hello. Pastor Wolfgang in Izmit introduced me to you, my name is Yunus Emre, I'm in Malatya and I'm looking for places with a church, could you assist me?" Necati apparently got the message and soon afterwards replied to Emre with a text message to his cell phone saying, "Emre, I'm Necati. I'm Wolfgang's brother-in-law; we have a place called Zirve distributors." Before long the electronic communications brought Emre and Necati face-to-face. They drank tea, chatted about Emre's college work and began to study the *Injil*. Necati had met dozens of other men from the same background and stage of life as Emre. Some he trusted more than others and though Necati had reservations about Emre's sincerity, he continued to show the young man love and concern, doing his best to discuss what it means to follow in the way of Jesus.

Several months prior to his contact with Necati, Emre had started to make acquaintances with the other young men. Hamit, Salih and Cuma lived in the same dormitory. For a while Emre had lived in their dormitory until he got into an argument with someone resulting in his expulsion. One day he visited the dormitory and took Salih aside to discuss the matter of missionary activity. Salih later claimed he knew little about missionary activity prior to his conversation with Emre. Emre allegedly described for him how the work of foreign and Turkish Christians across the country, including in and around Malatya, was in cooperation with the PKK, the Kurdish terrorist organization. Salih left with the impression that missionary activity was seditious, though Emre only offered his opinion with no hard evidence.

Around midnight one evening, Salih approached Cuma and Hamit in the dormitory while they were studying and invited them to the smoking lounge on the third floor. Emre was waiting for them. They sat down together and listened. Emre proceeded to describe a terrifying picture. Cuma later reported that Emre had warned them about the serious threat of missionaries. He frightened and angered them with warnings that the missionaries were planning to kill the children of people who wouldn't accept their faith. Cuma said Emre called upon everyone who loved his country and religion to do something about it. Was Emre joking or telling the truth? Sitting in the smoking lounge, the young men tried to decide. Emre would give them several more opportunities to see that he meant no joke.

Once Necati and Emre had established contact, they began to meet together talking about spiritual matters. Necati knew the content of the *Tevrat, Zebur, Injil* and the Qur'an very well. He was, after all, a *hafiz*, meaning someone who could chant the Qur'an from memory, and an educated Bible teacher. His conversations with Emre centered on the life and teachings of

Jesus. In the course of these meetings, Emre played the role of a sincere seeker to the degree that he said he was thinking about becoming a Christian.

In the period of a few weeks, Emre pressed to know more and more about Necati, Uğur, Tilmann and everyone else affiliated with the group of believers in Malatya. Along the way he became acquainted with Huseyin Yelki, a man claiming to be a Christian who volunteered at the Zirve office. Necati did not realize that in reality Yelki was passing along information to a number of government officials about the activities of Necati and Uğur and others in the small circle of believers in Malatya.

Emre learned that the believers met regularly in homes, so he asked to attend. Necati did not feel comfortable inviting him. Like many local people who believed the newspaper exaggerations, Emre thought Necati had helped establish fifty meetings in Malatya. Actually only two or three meetings met regularly in the city. In early spring Necati invited Emre to the celebration of Jesus' resurrection held at the *Altin Kayisi* (Golden Apricot) Hotel in Malatya. The date for the celebration was April 8, 2007. Tilmann prepared worship music that he led with his twelve-string guitar. A gifted worship leader and songwriter, he had written several worship songs in Turkish. The moderate-sized group gathered at the Altin Kayisi Hotel sang enthusiastically while little children played on the floor. The speaker proclaimed the death, burial and resurrection of Jesus the Messiah as foretold by the Old Testament prophets.

Before Emre arrived at Altin Kayisi, a couple of unidentified friends joined him. At the hotel reception an agitated Emre asked

for Necati. They directed him to the conference room where
the program had already started. He knocked on the door and
Uğur let him in. For about half an hour Emre and his friends
sat toward the back of the room watching and listening. Several
believers who were present remember seeing the young men with
dark countenances. Feeling disinterested and angry, they slipped
out the back door having only seen and heard a little.

A few days later Salih invited Cuma and Hamit to join him
with Emre at a tea house. When they arrived Emre took them
to the Kobra Kan martial arts center owned by his father. It was
locked but Emre had a key. The four men sat alone in the office
and talked over Emre's visit to the celebration at the Altin Kayisi
Hotel. Something had changed in him. He no longer wanted
to simply talk about the perceived missionary threat. After the
Altin Kayisi meeting Emre passionately reiterated his belief that
the missionaries posed a threat to the honor and religion of the
people. Emre insisted that something had to be done. He spoke
compellingly, *Something had to be done!* The time had come to act
against the missionaries, to uncover their work, to remove their
masks, to expose the powers behind them. The Kobra Kan center
became the center of operations for the men bent on attacking
the Christian believers. As the four men repeatedly met in the
Kobra Kan and other locations to discuss their plans, Emre
introduced the fifth man named Abuzer. The five young men
agreed together to do something about the missionaries.

Over the period of a few weeks, their conversations multiplied;
so did the number of cell phones in use. From late 2006 through
early 2007 Emre Gunaydin changed his cell phone 35 times. Salih
Gurler changed his 38 times and Hamit Ceker made 17 changes.

Emre used his multiple phones to make hundreds of calls in a network of shadowy links.

A week after the resurrection celebration, Salih, Cuma, Hamit, Abuzer and Emre met together in a café to discuss renting a car and taking action. Emre wanted everyone to contribute money toward the cost of the car rental. He said they would use the car to follow the missionaries hoping to learn more about their comings and goings. Cuma asked them to keep the meeting short since he had to do some studying. They quickly gathered the money. Emre announced that date had been set for them to move. They would act on April 16.

The Malatya church met on Sunday morning April 15. Uğur had not slept very well the night before. He had seen a troubling dream and didn't want to keep it to himself. During the meeting he said, "I want to share with the rest of you a dream I had last night. I think maybe God wants to tell us something through it, but I don't know exactly what." The others sat quietly in the living room, waiting to hear what he might say, trusting God to direct them. Uğur continued to speak. "In my dream, something terrible happened. It was very distressing and I still feel upset from it. Whatever it was that happened, it changed everything. I mean, everything changed afterwards."

Someone asked, "Uğur would you like us to pray for you about this dream?"

"Yes," he said, "I would like your prayers."

They prayed together, "Yes Lord, you see your child Uğur

and know everything there is to know about him and about this dream that he saw last night. We ask you to give him your strength to face whatever each day brings. We ask for your strength to face whatever changes may come our way. Thank you for your constant presence and support, in the Name of Jesus, amen."

April 16 approached, bringing lovely spring weather to the fertile valleys and city streets, preparing the land for the next harvest of apricots. People put up signs around town indicating the week of *Kutlu Dogum Haftasi*—the Celebrated Week of Muhammad's Birthday. Meanwhile, the five young men learned that Necati was out of town, so they postponed their attack until April 18. On Tuesday the 17th, Emre, Salih and Abuzer purchased three guns that fired blanks and one box of blank bullets. After getting a bite to eat, they cruised around town looking for a place to test fire the weapons. After being stopped by the traffic police, they managed to find a secluded place where they thought they could test the weapons unnoticed. They fired about 30 rounds, then drove back into town. Police stopped them at the Battalgazi Boulevard. It seemed that some complaints had been made about their firing the weapons and they asked to see the receipt of purchase. Wanting to ask more questions, police took them to the station. However, other than having to pay a small fine, nothing else happened.

At eight in the evening Hamit came to Cuma and took him out to meet the other three. They arrived in a rented sedan, drove around together and stopped to get sandwiches. Cuma had spent the last couple of days with his parents who were not feeling well, so he had missed the latest plans. While Hamit and Abuzer got out of the car to get the sandwiches, Salih suggested they tell Cuma the latest. They finished their food and drove to a nearby market where they purchased five knives, five pairs of plastic gloves and five *cevsen*, triangle-shaped leather pouches containing portions of the Qur'an. They had purchased clothesline earlier. Wanting to rest before getting up early the next morning, Salih, Hamit and Cuma dropped off Abuzer and Emre and drove back to the dormitory.

At some point that evening, Emre made arrangements with a young man named Mehmet for him to copy and examine hard drive files they planned to steal the next day from the Zirve offices. Mehmet agreed he would look at the hard drive and he would wait for Emre's signal the next morning.

Cell phone records give a detailed glimpse into Emre's final hours leading up to the morning of April 18. At 22:44 Emre sent a text message to his girlfriend Turna: *"Turna, what's up, are you okay? Tomorrow absolutely do not call me … could you pray for me? … don't worry about me, nothing will happen, Allah willing, I'll live for another thirty years."*

Someone called Özbacim sent a message to Emre at 22:46. *"Aren't you at home brother, why don't you answer?"* At 22:55 he wrote, *"… May Allah be your helper brother, watch yourself."* After several more cell message exchanges, Turna wrote at 00:08, *"Emre, is there something you haven't told me or you failed to mention?"*

The morning of April 18 dawned early for Emre and his friends. At 06:44 he sent off a text to Turna saying, *"Come on Turna, trust in Allah and pray, okay."* At 06:48 he wrote a message to "Ciger" and said, "*Brother, in five minutes we will get Abuzer.*" At 06:57 he sent a message to "Mavis", "*Brother, we'll be there in ten minutes.*"

Turna replied to Emre at 07:00. "*You keep your trust in Allah too, he's the greatest magnificence for all things, don't forget to send me news.*"

"*You really take care of yourself*" At 7:03 she wrote, "*Allah willing ... this is the day you will eat the macaroni.*" At 7:07, "*Okay, but really really watch out for yourself ... in God's way we will meet again in a short time.*" Emre replied at 7:07 and said, "*Don't worry.*"

The text conversation between Emre and his girlfriend went deeper. At 7:14 he wrote, "*Offer your last rites, forgiving anything, whatever happens.*" She replied immediately, "*Ohhh, nothing will happen, Allah willing. But still, I'll say last rites for you. And if anything happens to me, say them for me too.*"

The men had arranged to meet early in the morning and travel in the rental car together to the Ağbaba office center where according to their testimonies, they would attempt to tie up the men and ransack their office in search of hard evidence to prove missionaries were bent on destroying the country. Emre planned to quickly transport the stolen CDs and computer hardware to his friend.

Around eight o'clock the men started their eventful day with breakfast at a spacious tea house directly opposite the Ağbaba offices. They sat on short stools and huddled around a low table. Everything looked perfectly normal with five local guys dressed in casual clothes of jeans, light jackets, and sports shoes chatting together while they downed hot tea and bread. Having concealed their knives, guns, gloves, ropes and towels somewhere else, nothing about their appearance gave away any hint of their dark plans.

Necati had been out of town at a conference for several days doing some teaching and study. Having just gotten back from the long trip, he felt he could hardly pull himself out of the bed and away from his wife and children that morning. Furthermore, Necati continued to feel somewhat troubled about Emre and didn't quite know what to think. No one knew better than Necati the strange, erroneous, even dangerous kinds of things that some of his fellow countrymen thought about Christians. He had been harassed and arrested so many times he had lost count. Even his own family of origin had rejected him, so he knew it was entirely possible that Emre and his friends meant him no good. And though Necati, Uğur and Tilmann had repeated endlessly that they loved Turkey, they were sober enough to realize that the words would often fall upon deaf ears. Still, he wanted Emre and other young men like him to hear the good news of forgiveness and eternal life in Messiah Jesus. So though it was hard for many reasons to get dressed and leave for the office the morning of April 18, Necati got out of bed, dressed, read his Bible, prayed with his wife, then stepped into the busy streets of downtown Malatya.

Of the three Christians men, Tilmann had the least interaction with Emre and his four friends headed toward the Zirve office. First, he didn't work for Zirve himself, but simply rented office space from them. Secondly, as a Turkish-speaking German, he knew that Necati and Uğur, being local Turkish believers, could relate with other Turks more naturally than he could. That morning he had some accounting business to take care of at the office, so he dressed, kissed Susanne and left. The last thing he said on the way out was, "I love you."

Emre and his friends finished their tea and food, paid the bill and made their way over to the Ağbaba office building. It was still fairly early. They climbed the dark stairwell to the third floor where Zirve had a rented office and knocked on the door. No one answered so they returned outside for ten minutes or so before trying again. Still, no one came to the door, so they piled into the car and drove around Malatya. At a mosque they stopped to use the toilets, then decided to go over to the Kobra Kan sports center. Emre had a key and opened the center. They talked and drank coffee trying to pass the time. Someone suggested they do their morning prayers, called the *rekat namaz,* in pairs. Each man, as he had been taught from youth, ritually washed himself in preparation for the prayers. After prayers Emre suggested they each write a letter to his family as a record explaining why they were about to attack the Zirve office. One by one they took paper and a pen to write out their thoughts. The notes were short but to the point.

One simply penned a few simple words saying, *"This is surely a day."*

Another wrote,

My dear Mother, My dear Father. I love you very much, but my love for Allah and my love for the country have involved me in this path. May you think about this correctly, because I haven't done anything wrong. I've done this for my religion and my flag. If anything happens to me, may everything be well for you and the country, because our great honor is our country. Allah willing, I will embrace you with my right and left. My Allah bless you and our gain. Allah willing, our religion will reach the next generations. May our country be strong.

Someone else said,

My dear Family and my dear love. I've entered this path, maybe you will be angry with me, but in my heart is Allah, my country and your love, your lovely rose, I've entered this path with MUCH loving happiness. Don't be angry with me, the greatest honor for a person or the greatest honor for me is in my country and I'm filled with the love of Allah. I've died in Allah's love. May our country be strong and you be strong my love.

Another note said,

My dear Mother and only Father. My bright eyed sisters, don't cry for me. For you, your country, for you Allah, only Love, I've started this path. I'm very happy. I love you.

In another note someone wrote,

Mother, Father, Brothers, I love you more than everything else in the world. Why does a person live? For honor, a good reputation, for the country. We are the sons of Turks, truly Turk ... please say the forgiveness rites for me, I want nothing else. I've lived for Allah, I'll die for Allah, I'm not afraid of death. May God's love not diminish in me. Allahu Akbar.

Yet another one penned, "*May Allah protect and exalt the Turks. Amen*."

After expressing on paper their motivations for going to the Zirve office, the men discussed their next steps. This time they decided to go not as a group, but separately. Emre and Abuzer would go up to the office first. When they felt ready, Emre would send a text to Salih, Hamit and Cuma who would be waiting just outside on the street below. At 9:18 Mehmet sent Emre a text message from the computer shop, "*I've come just now.*"

Emre replied, "*Brother, we went twice to the grocery, it wasn't open. When it opens, I'll get the fruit and other things and come to you, just stay open, I'll bring the vegetables and other things, okay.*" A few minutes later Mehmet answered, saying "*I'm at the store nephew, send and come.*"

Sometime after ten o'clock in the morning the five men arrived in the car on a side street near the Ağbaba office building. While still sitting in the car, they divided up the knives and guns. They also took out the ropes, gloves and towels. Hamit, Cuma and Abuzer each took a gun.

Emre and Abuzer went to the office first. On the way up the dark corridor, Emre took the gun from Abuzer so he would have it in the event that Abuzer had to leave for some reason and he was left alone with Necati, Uğur and Tilmann. They gathered at the Zirve door and rang the bell. This time they heard noise from inside. Uğur opened the door and warmly welcomed them into the main office. Tilmann and his accountant friend were working quietly in another room. Shortly afterwards the accountant left.

Uğur offered the young men tea and comfortable seats in front of Necati's desk. Still hoping that Emre had some sincere interest in discussing the *Injil*, Uğur opened the subject. For about fifteen minutes the three men chatted. Uğur may have noticed that Emre seemed a bit preoccupied with his cell phone. At 10:53 Emre texted a message to Salih, "*There are three apples here, we're drinking tea, when I've given the news, come up and let's eat them together.*"

Mehmet at the electronics store was getting impatient. At 11:03 he wrote Emre, "*Brother, where are you, the food is getting cold, I'm waiting for you, our people are curious about you, anyway, I give you my kisses.*"

Around this time Emre excused himself to use the toilet. At 11:04 Emre texted Salih. "*Come on, let's eat the apples together.*"

This was the signal the other three had been waiting for. Salih, Hamit, and Cuma approached the office building one at a time. They all gathered closely at the Zirve office door. Salih rang the bell. Uğur jumped up and opened the door to the three men. Salih asked, "May we speak to Necati Bey?" Emre followed Uğur to the door and quickly introduced Hamit, Salih and Cuma as his friends who were also interested in learning more about Christianity. Uğur showed the three new men to their seats and offered them tea as well. Tilmann came in for a few moments while Emre went around the circle introducing everyone. "This is Hamit, Cuma, Salih and Abuzer." The five settled into the guest chairs in the main office, nervously exchanging glances. Uğur's cell phone rang and he excused himself, explaining he had to go downstairs for a moment. In Uğur's absence, Tilmann sat down to entertain the five guests. He introduced himself and spoke to Emre, "Yes, I think I may have seen you at the Resurrection Celebration meeting at the Altin Kayisi Hotel."

The doorbell rang again. Tilmann excused himself and opened the door. The five men whispered among themselves, some expressing doubts about staying while the others said they shouldn't leave. This time Necati, Uğur and Tilmann returned to the main room with a cargo deliveryman. He dropped off a package and quickly left. Tilmann excused himself from the group and went back to his office. Necati, smiling brightly as normal, welcomed the five young men to the office. Perhaps he felt excited to see such a large group of young men claiming they wanted to learn more about the *Injil*. Or did he sense some kind of nervousness or tenseness among them? Could they look him in the eye?

Necati checked their tea cups and offered to pour more for anyone who wanted it. With Necati now present, Emre became more aggressive in his questions about the Christian faith. He asked, "What do you really believe, what kind of books do you read, do you believe in Jesus, what books are the foundation of your faith?" Necati was never known to become easily flustered. He could handle difficult and sensitive questions with patience and thoughtfulness. In his reply to Emre he tried to restate some of the same things he had said in their recent conversations and lessons: Christians believe the Bible is reliable and unchanged, it teaches that Jesus was more than a prophet, that he was God who had come in the form of a sinless man to die on the cross as a sacrifice for our sins. The conversation grew hotter. On the one hand, Emre wanted to defend Islam. On the other, Necati continued to plead with the men that God offers eternal life through faith in Jesus the Messiah. Emre pressed harder, "Anyway, what's the difference between Christianity and Islam, what does it matter if we became Christians, how would it benefit us?"

Noon was now approaching. Emre went to the toilet again. This time, instead of his cell phone, he took in his hand a gleaming, razor-sharp knife. He stepped back into the main room, his eyes wild with rage. Before anyone could react he grabbed Uğur, pressing the knife to his throat. In a flurry of motion, guns and knives came into the open, threatening Necati and Uğur. Necati cried out, fear choking his voice, "No, this is not the way!"

Tilmann heard troubling noises in the next room, so he left his desk to see what was happening. Entering the main room he saw the five men wielding knives and guns. They quickly subdued him.

In those first few seconds when the knives and guns first came out, Tilmann and Necati saw not just the faces of their attackers, they must have seen those of their wives and children. Uğur thought of his fiancée, as well as the families of his two close friends now being accosted next to him. Had there been any way of resisting or escaping, they would have certainly tried to return safely to their loved ones.

Like crazed demons Emre and Salih screamed at the men to get face down on the floor. There was more pushing and shoving and someone delivered a severe blow to Necati's head. They bound the men hand and foot while they lay on the floor, tightening the cords until they cut into their skin stopping circulation. Emre reportedly said to Necati, "Lie down on the floor and say the *Shahada* (Islamic confession of faith), I'm going to make you a Muslim." While Emre went to the toilet and cut a towel into pieces, Abuzer said to Necati, "So Jesus is the Messiah? He's God?! There is no Messiah or God, only Allah."

Emre returned with the towels. They gagged Tilmann and Necati, who by then may or may not have been conscious. Emre started questioning Uğur. "Who do you work for, what's your purpose, what people are behind you?" At that moment the doorbell rang, interrupting their plans. One of the startled men looked through the peep-hole and saw a Turkish man and woman standing in the hallway. Again and again the couple rang the bell and knocked. They also tried to open the door from the outside with a key, but the assailants had used a key on the inside of the door to lock it, prohibiting the exterior lock from working. Uğur's cell phone began to ring repeatedly. Finally a desperate Emre told Uğur to answer the phone. "Tell them to go to the Altin Kayisi Hotel," he ordered, "and meet you there, and that your battery is out, you'll talk to them later." Moments later a couple of the young men went to the balcony and spotted the same couple looking upwards from the sidewalk. Some of them became frightened, but Emre warned them there was no turning back.

The attack became more vicious. The men stabbed the razor-sharp kitchen knives into Necati's, Tilmann's and Uğur's immobilized bodies stretched on the floor in front of the low table where their cups still sat half-filled with warm tea. They kicked and beat them with vicious blows. They stabbed deeply into their upper bodies, sometimes not only stabbing but twisting the knives, making the men writhe and moan in agony. Over and over they dug their blades into living human flesh, cursing and ranting wildly to verbally abuse the three Christians in any way possible.

The three men were lying so closely to one another on the office floor they nearly touched. The blows and stabs made their blood splatter on the floor, the furniture, the walls and the killers' clothes. Their lives ebbed with the steady flow of blood. Tilmann's face began to swell and puff with dark purplish bruises. Necati's head had been disfigured. Uğur moaned and trembled on the floor, calling out in a weak voice, "*Isa Mesih*." While streams of blood from the three Christians soaked everything in the room and mingled in one pool in their final moments, Emre screamed hideously, "These bloodless people would kill our children!" He then yelled, "Salih, take something and choke Necati and kill him." Salih took a piece of cord and tried to kill Necati by pulling it around his neck but was unable to stop his breathing. Emre grabbed a knife and knelt down beside Necati. From reports it seems likely that he was the one who slashed the knife blade across his neck, slicing through his blood vessels and esophagus as though slaughtering sacrificial sheep. A fountain of blood squirted out while Necati's heart beat the last few times. Liters of dark red blood quickly pooled on the floor next to his twitching body. With a last gasp of breath he departed this life.

Next they moved to Tilmann. Again, it was probably Emre who took his knife to slit his throat while Salih, the largest of the five, held Tilmann still. Blood gushed over the floor while the man of peaceful and quiet character took a last gasp of air and then went still.

Uğur remained alive. He continued breathing, though he felt weak and in agony from stab wounds and blows. After he heard the sounds of his friends dying, he became still and quiet. In his heart he felt the greatest agony. Emre said, "We're not going to kill you, but take you with us." He covered Uğur's head with a towel while others began to stab Uğur in the back. One of them at the window shouted that the couple who was waiting on the sidewalk had called the police. Uğur mustered his strength and cried out, "Help, help!" Emre quickly put a towel in his mouth to stifle his cries. Panicking from the possible arrival of the police, someone grabbed a knife and hastily slashed it across Uğur's throat, but not with the precision that was used on Necati and Tilmann. This time, though blood rushed onto the floor, Uğur continued hanging on to life.

Rushing now against time, Emre, Hamit, and Abuzer rummaged through Necati's, Uğur's and Tilmann's desks, looking for some kind of evidence to support their suspicions that missionaries and Christians posed a grave danger to their country. Christian books, booklets, CDs and lessons covered the modest bookshelves, desks and book carousel in the Zirve office. Tilmann's office contained a few documents in German which caught their attention, but they were only mundane legal documents. They searched the pockets and wallets of the men, perhaps hoping to find money and examined their computers, taking Necati's flash drive. A few moments later the police arrived at the door and began knocking.

The couple that had arrived at the Zirve office door was Gorkhan and his wife, the ones who had moved to Malatya to take the place of the South Africans who had to leave. It puzzled and worried them that their office key didn't work and no one would open the door from the inside. At that time of day someone should be there. They suspected something seriously wrong. None of it made sense. They went back downstairs and tried to look up to the office from the sidewalk, but couldn't ascertain what was happening inside. The phone call to Uğur only deepened Gorkhan's concern and fear. Something was wrong, very wrong. Uğur's trembling and weak voice couldn't disguise his terror. And why would he say go to the Altin Kayisi Hotel? Gorkhan tried not to think the worse but he knew he must do something, and quickly, so he dialed the police emergency number 155. The following is the transcript of the conversation starting at 12:52, April 18, 2007.

Operator: 155, Police assistance.

Caller (Gorkhan): Good day, sir.

O: Good day, how can I help you?

C: I want to make a notification.

O: About what?

C: I can't reach my friends.

O: What do you mean you can't reach them?

C: I mean all morning I haven't been able to reach them then a little bit ago I spoke with one on the phone, he sounded worried, like he wanted to hide something.

O: How did he sound worried?

C: I mean he said, 'I'm not at all at work, I'm somewhere else.' For example, he spoke in a very low voice then he hung up the phone abruptly but I really want to have the office checked.

O: What kind of check do you want?

C: I want to have their work office checked.

O: Where are they?

C: The third floor of the Ağbaba office building.

O: Where is the Ağbaba office building?

C: It's behind the Niyazi Misri Mosque, I'm also at the office and have a key that I've tried but the door won't open.

O: Niyazi Misri boulevard Agbaba office building third floor.

C: Yes, I'm there now for that matter.

O: Your work place is there?

C: Yes, Zirve Publishers

O: Zirve Publishers?

C: Yes

O: Who are the people?

C: One is Uğur Yuksel, another is Necati Aydin, one is named Tilmann Geske.

O: Why are you suspicious now?

C: I mean, I don't know, normally we talk, but I haven't been able to reach them for a long time.

O: Okay, are you in front of the Ağbaba office building now?

C: Yes, I'm normally there at my office.

O: Okay, I'm sending a squad there now, you can meet with your friends.

C: Okay.

At 12:54 the police arranged to go to the Zirve office. The following is the transcript of the police conversation.

Center: 4830

4830: Roger, Center

C: Niyazi Mirsi boulevard Ağbaba office building third floor …

in the Zirve Publishers are some people who aren't responding, someone called 155 and is waiting in front of the office, it would be appropriate to meet a squad, okay.

4830: Understood, Center, 4850

4850: We're passing over.

4850: Center, 4830, at the place, we'll check it out and give info.

4830: Understood.

4850: Center

C: Go ahead.

4850—It would be good to call emergency for Niyazi Mirsi boulevard Ağbaba office building.

C: Understood, okay, let's talk on the telephone.

4850—Understood, okay.

4830: Center, 4850, I'm nearby, do you need reinforcements?

4850—Negative for now.

At 13:07 a call was made to 155 Police assistance.

Operator: 155 police help.

3852: 3852, sir, at the identified location someone has fallen down from the balcony.

O: From where?

3852: If there's an ambulance, they fell here at the Ağbaba office center.

O: Where's an ambulance, okay I'll send one.

3852: It'll be really good if it's fast.

O: Did he commit suicide?

3852: He fell, nothing's clear yet, the ambulance should come very quickly.

O: okay.

Another call went through at 13:09

O: 155

4850: This is the police officer Savas.

O : Savas

4850—We're at the Zirve Publishers.

O: Yes

4850: There's three people inside, I don't know the total number of people, two or three more people, I mean one jumped from the balcony and fell to the ground, the third is laying down in front of the door, the other two are probably inside, some others already.

O: Okay, it's been said three people are inside, did they throw the person or maybe did he jump himself?

4850: If I guess, they're thieves.

O: One of the persons is a German.

4850: The man with us who works with Zirve said that the one who fell is not one of his co-workers and he doesn't recognize him.

O: Inside is Uğur Yuksel, Necati Aydin and a German Wilyim Geyst, like that.

4850: They won't open the door.

O: They aren't opening the door?

4850—Yes, they aren't opening the door.

O: Talk to the commissioner, if not, if it's needed, open the door with a locksmith.

4850—Okay.

By this time the police had climbed the stairs to the third floor with Gorkhan. They tried in vain to open the door, continuously talking over the radio trying to decide what to do next. Suddenly the door opened from the inside. Hamit stood before them, covered in blood. He, Cuma and Salih had decided to surrender to the police. Abuzer had attempted to escape out the balcony just off of Tilmann's room. It was too difficult to climb down, so he re-entered the office. Emre followed Abuzer out and tried to get down from the balcony but he lost his footing and plunged three stories to the concrete sidewalk below. He hit the ground instantly losing consciousness.

The police ordered the four young men to sit on the floor and handcuffed them. They entered the main office. There the police and Gorkhan witnessed a scene of horror unequaled in modern Turkish history. Necati's mutilated body lay lifeless in a pool of blood on the left side of the room in front of Uğur's desk. He had died first. Directly left of the door parallel to the wall lay Tilmann's tall frame, the floor around him soaked in blood. Uğur lay in a puddle of blood in front of the door parallel to the wall on the right. Amazingly, he could still just breathe through his slit throat. Blood covered everything. The killers had walked through the blood, leaving footprints everywhere. The scene was an unspeakable, unforgettable picture of the worse kind of suffering one human can inflict upon another.

Gorkhan, a fellow believer and good friend of Necati, Uğur and Tilmann looked on the incomprehensible scene of death with utter shock. He stumbled back downstairs to the entrance of the Ağbaba office building. When the police escorted the killers out of the building, he became hysterical with anger and grief and tried to throttle one of the killers. Police held him back and prevented him from hurting anyone. He later confessed he knew he had done the wrong thing and expressed sorrow that he had been unable to cope with his shock and anger.

Ambulances and television crews arrived on the scene simultaneously. Crowds gathered along the sidewalks, streets and children's park just in front of the office building. Traffic paralyzed the Niyazi Misiri Boulevard as officials reacted hastily to deal with the carnage. At the speed of light, disturbing images of the deaths swept across Turkey and to the rest of the world. A journalist snapped a close-up photo of Abuzer's dark eyes glancing sideways as a police officer held his coat tightly and moved him toward a secure vehicle. The television cameras captured real-time images of emergency personnel struggling to push their way through the crowds of police and journalists with the heavy weight of a dead human body in a black plastic bag, as though someone might carry out the trash. First one body, then another. The shoes on their feet revealed the men's identity to friends and acquaintances watching the dreadful drama unfold before their eyes.

The medical personnel then came out of the building carrying Uğur, still alive and conscious in spite of his stab wounds and viciously gashed throat. As they moved him from the entrance of the Ağbaba office building to the open doors of the waiting ambulance, he weakly waved his hand toward the gaping gash across his neck.

Unlike the others, Uğur would live for several more hours while doctors attempted to do the impossible by stitching the slit throat and replenishing gallons of blood lost from his wounds. In those final hours he not only suffered the pain of his wounds, but the mental anguish of knowing that he was slowly dying for a crime he never committed, killed by young men whom he had tried to befriend. He had ample time to think about the profound grief Necati's wife, son and daughter would experience for the rest of their lives when they learned what had just happened in the Zirve office, right before his own eyes. When he remembered Tilmann's smile, his wife's bubbly personality and his three lovely children, he mourned over the heartache he knew they would always live with. Of the three men who suffered so much, Uğur would suffer the most, carrying the heaviest spiritual burden in those last hours while he searched the unfamiliar faces of medics, doctors and nurses, remembering his parents, friends and the land of his birth and childhood, life and death.

In those final hours, while the clock ticked ever so slowly, had the fatal gash not stolen his ability to speak, Uğur might have echoed the words of the first Christian martyr killed 2000 years earlier, "Lord Jesus, receive my spirit … lay not this sin to their charge." And like Stephen, "when he said this, he fell asleep."

 # Tell Me! Is He Dead or Alive?

B y noon Susanne thought the morning was going very strangely. Things made her feel worried and maybe a little angry. Tilmann said he had some work at the office, but when she tried to call him, he didn't answer. Not only that, but the answering service came on. That was very strange; he never turned his phone off. So what was going on? Her anxiety grew over the next couple of hours. By two o'clock she still hadn't reached Tilmann. Then her phone rang. Shemse's voice poured out, sounding distraught. She said that someone from Izmir had called asking if she was all right. But why wouldn't she be all right? Neither of the women had seen the news, they had no inkling about the events transpiring just across town at the Zirve office. News reports said something tragic had happened. Shemse didn't know what to say, neither did Susanne, but fear of the worst filled the hearts of both wondering wives. Where were their husbands? What was going on?

Feelings of helplessness and urgency increased as the news reports gave conflicting information. One of Susanne's neighbors came to her home and said she had heard a Canadian was killed in Malatya at an office near the Zirve office. But that didn't make sense, if there was a Canadian in a town the size of Malatya, Susanne would likely know about him. The misinformation did not bode well. Somehow a rumor reached her that a Turk named Emre and a foreigner wearing a cross had been taken to the hospital. Tilmann didn't wear a cross. Later they learned that the man with the cross was Uğur and that the police therefore assumed he was a foreigner ... after all, didn't everyone know that a Turk would never be caught dead or alive in a cross?

Phone calls from friends and acquaintances multiplied. Everyone hoped Susanne knew something, since it appeared her husband was involved in the event. But she couldn't say anything conclusively; she still had no confirmation of Tilmann's whereabouts or his condition. It seemed possible that he might be alive somewhere, perhaps he was injured or taken hostage, she had no way of knowing how he was. Still, the calls continued from friends offering their sympathies and help. One caller expressed sorrow about Tilmann's death. Tilmann ... dead?! She cried out and hung up the phone. Desperate to know the truth, she gathered up Lukas and Miriam and rushed to the local hospital.

Susanne seated Lukas and Miriam as comfortably as she could in the unadorned hospital waiting room. The place buzzed with police chattering on cell phones, taking notes and talking in hushed conversations. Susanne waited for news, but none was forthcoming. The children became bored and restless and asked about their father. Susanne felt as though she would burst under the pressure of the circumstances. Finally, in a last desperate attempt to learn the condition of her husband, she threw open the waiting room doors and seized one of the policemen by the jacket. "Tell me what you know," she demanded, "tell me if my husband is dead or alive."[10] For a moment the officer communicated only with his eyes, but it was enough for Susanne as she gazed intently at him. She asked again, "Is he dead?"

"Yes," the man said.

Across town in her apartment, Shemse finally heard confirmation of Necati's death. Overcome with emotion she fell to her knees and wept. She also had to tell Esther and Elisha. They wept together. The tears flowed and flowed, a well that would never completely run dry. Necati was larger than life. He was Elisha's hero, Esther's loving heart and Shemse's sunlight. His untiring smile brightened all their lives like no other. The little ones remembered their dad going away on trips when he would meet with people to talk about Jesus and deliver material for Zirve. Sometimes he would go away for several days, but he always came back and when he did, what a wonderful reunion they would have. They hugged and kissed and wrestled on the floor. The kids climbed all over him as though he was a big, affectionate bear. Shemse would sit and watch, her eyes sparkling and her heart filled with joy. Each day she thanked God for their marriage and their home, knowing that it was a special gift, that Necati was a special gift not only to her, but many other people as well. In the days following Necati's bloody death for his Christian faith, he became a gift to the whole nation, his story sealed in history. If this was God's will for Necati in the cause of following Jesus, Shemse would say yes to God. But still, it hurt to lose him, it hurt so badly and deeply, she knew she could only endure by the power of God.

Uğur's fiancée, family and friends struggled to manage their grief and loss. This bright, philosophical son of the East was snuffed out by people who had completely misunderstood him and his work. He had been denied the chance to marry and have children. So much of his life stretched before him, a life that would have taken him into wonderful possibilities, but now it would not be. Few men exhibited humility and Christlikeness as Uğur. He had chosen to accept the risks and even willingly put himself into a dangerous situation. He had shown love for his fellow Turks, though some had rejected that love and some had chosen to respond with violence and murder. "No greater love has anyone than this, than he lay down his life for his friends."

Wonderful Indeed

The nation and world immediately reacted to the murders while the families tried to get through each moment. The press overwhelmed Malatya and the widows. The families made plans for the funerals. Shemse and friends arranged to have Necati transported by air to Izmir, where they would bury him in a small Christian cemetery. As Necati's widow, she had the legal power to override his family's request to bury him according to Islamic rites. Representatives from Turkey's small Christian community and members of the press attended Necati's funeral.

Uğur's family chose to bury him just outside his hometown of Elazığ in the boundless steppe of eastern Turkey. His father personally instructed the tombstone engraver to write, "He died like Jesus."

Susanne requested permission to have Tilmann buried in Malatya. Even though he was not a Turkish citizen, Tilmann had given his life for the people and the land, ultimately dying for his Lord. Burial sites and rites are a very sensitive subject for Muslims. Yet Susanne insisted that the Turkish government find a place to bury him. They finally granted permission to place him in a small, dusty cemetery Armenian Christians had used on the edge of Malatya. In Turkey he would stay until the end.

Scores of family, friends, journalists, officials and on-lookers turned out on the day of Tilmann's funeral hoping to hear what Susanne had to say. Since the murders she had hesitated to speak to the press. She was exhausted and traumatized, but Christian friends encouraged her that perhaps this was a moment God had given her to lift up the name of Jesus before a watching world, not only in Turkey but in countless other places and languages. She thought and prayed about their encouragement, finally deciding that, yes, she would put some thoughts down on paper. When the press conference convened, writers and cameramen jostled for a good position to see Susanne. She felt nervous and weak. God would have to be her strength in this moment. She began reading her statement to the silent and motionless crowd.

> We came to this country to live a normal life, the same as the Turks come to Germany as Muslims. We wanted to come to Turkey and live here as Christians. For us this is a very hard time, I have lost my lifelong friend and the children have lost their father. But I know that Tilmann died as a martyr in the name of Jesus Christ. His blood was not in vain. For Malatya and for Turkey this is a new start. Jesus said from the cross to the people around him,

"Father, forgive them, for they know not what they do" and I want to do the same.[11]

Shemse took a similar approach, declaring at Necati's funeral in front of national and international press, "We forgive them because Jesus forgave us." She added, "I know my Necati was praying for them, even while he was being tortured."[12]

In the days and weeks after the funeral, the media mob gradually dwindled, bringing relief to Susanne and her family. Countless friends and guests had stayed close by, but even their numbers dropped off little by little, allowing the Geskes to slowly start a routine and adjust to being a family again, trying to live in Malatya without Tilmann. One evening Susanne and the children sat around together, enjoying being alone. They had just finished supper and were making a treat. Something was bothering Miriam. "Mom," she said, "can I ask you something?"

"Of course, honey, what would you like to ask?" Susanne replied.

"You know how you went on the television and all the newspapers and everybody talked about how you forgave the men that killed Daddy?"

"Yes, that's what I did, it's what Jesus wants me to do, and it's what Daddy would have wanted me to do too."

"Yes, but they did such a terrible thing," she paused, her little eyes tearing up. "Daddy's with Jesus but we don't have him anymore, and I miss him so much."

Susanne reached down and took her little girl in her arms. "My love, we do miss him, we all miss him, it hurts I know."

"But how can we just forgive those men? I don't feel like forgiving them, I feel angry about it."

Susanne sat down with Miriam on her lap, while the other two children joined them at the dinner table sitting together. "I know it is hard to understand. It is hard to forgive, and from a natural point of view, it doesn't make much sense. Part of us wants life to be fair. We want people who do bad things to be punished. In the Old Testament the law taught an eye for an eye and a tooth for a tooth."

Miriam looked up with her wide eyes and said, "What does that mean?"

"It meant that whatever wrong one person did to someone else, the same thing would be done to them. If someone injured another person's eye, the first person would have his own eye injured. Or if someone knocked a tooth out of someone else's mouth, he would have his own tooth knocked out. It sounds rather harsh, I know."

Lukas joined in, "And I guess that means someone who kills someone should be killed."

Susanne said, "Yes, that was their way. God takes sin seriously. But Jesus made a way for us to forgive and leave the punishment up to him. These men did a terrible thing to your father, to Uncle Uğur and to Uncle Necati. We can't bring them back, but they are living peacefully now in heaven with God." She paused and then added, "But what we can do is forgive them from our hearts. Because Jesus died on the cross and suffered for everyone, we can forgive."

Michal looked at her mother and said, "So Jesus went through even more suffering than Daddy did."

"And he was with Daddy through it all, he never left his side, he was right there with all the men, supporting them in ways that we will never know, just as he is with us now."

Miriam said, "I believe he is with us, maybe he can help us forgive and maybe we can tell those men that he died on the cross for them too. They can believe and be forgiven. That would be wonderful, wouldn't it?"

"Yes," Susanne said, "that would be very wonderful indeed."

 # Friends Remember

Sometime after the deaths several of Necati's, Uğur's and Tilmann's friends had the opportunity to share their intimate thoughts and feelings about the three men. They eagerly offered their memories for this story. The warm and personal conversations brought back smiles and laughs mingled with many tears.

Sali, a good friend and co-worker described Necati. "He was a great evangelist and I especially would like to point out that everywhere he went he loved to talk to people about God's Word and he didn't just stay in one place but continually went out wanting to spread the good news. He was always visiting people and giving lessons with his brothers, he loved studying the Injil. He loved discipling people. He was very courageous and wasn't afraid. He used to say that in this world we didn't have any rest, but that our rest would come in the heavenly Jerusalem. I also want to stress that he didn't just spread the good news in word but also through his willingness to assist people in their physical needs. He gathered clothes and assistance and took a work group to restore a school in Malatya, I think it made a big impression on Malatya."

Offering a fresh perspective about the reaction in Turkey a young friend of the martyrs named Tarkan said, "We all expressed our deepest condolences to the families. At one of the book fairs where we opened a book stand many strangers just stopped by and offered their apologies and sorrow for what happened. They were very angry at the five men who committed this crime. Some commented that Muslims are opening mosques in Europe and America but when someone here distributes the Injil they are stabbed. It really encouraged us that people would stop by and offer their support like that. It was a great thing."

Farhat, a strong Turkish leader in the church was closely involved with the events of April 18 and related his experiences.

He said, "On the day of the murders I was working in another city. Around noon I visited a friend and at one o'clock as we were wrapping up, I got a telephone call. They said confusing news about a bomb going off in the Malatya office. We immediately got in our car and took off straight for Malatya since we were already so close. We cried as we were driving there, we just couldn't believe it. We felt if only we could have been there one second earlier, if only we could have reached them one second earlier, of course there is nothing we could have done, but we felt that way in our hearts. We prayed and cried."

"I stayed three days there," he continued. "After the deaths the brothers said, 'We mustn't close this office, we will press on, we're not better than our brothers but we must press on.' Two days later we went to the morgue and with our own hands covered our brothers' bodies with a burial shroud and prepared their coffins. Necati's body went to Izmir where he was buried at the church with a funeral ceremony. When our brothers died there we felt extreme suffering but we weren't afraid and we're not afraid because God has strengthened us."

"I miss everything about them," said Mahmut. "Their voices still ring in my ears. During a period of two years Necati and I stayed in the same hotel room on ministry trips. We breathed the same air. In the same way I roomed with Uğur breathing the same air. We traveled together in the same car and worked together. I miss everything."

A believer from outside Turkey reflected on how the deaths impacted him and Christians around the world. He said,

"While visiting in the US I was surprised at how far and wide the news of the murders had traveled across America. I often feel like few people really understand what this country is like. But I was surprised at how much interest people there showed in what was happening here and it was encouraging. One thing is that this is a call to prayer. I remember telling people, 'you know, these men died because of lies. They died because they were thought to be men that they weren't.' God never promises us safety, he really doesn't. Following Jesus is not about safety. It's about obedience. I think in the West, sure we're afraid of Islam. But we shouldn't be afraid. Isn't that what Jesus tells us? We shouldn't be afraid of those who can kill the body but we should fear the one who can throw our souls into hell. It's difficult for the average Western to understand. It's generally what we don't know that we are most afraid of. I just encourage people to pray."

Ali, was close to the men said, "I can say that meeting men like Necati and Uğur was a turning point in my life and I thank God for every day I spent with them. Like Necati told me one day in sincerity, 'I love you,' I want to reply, 'I also love you Necati. I love you my brother Uğur.'"

 # World Reactions

The events of April 18, 2007 sparked many top-level reactions from within Turkey and then from around the world. The Turkish government made statements and started investigations. The German embassy requested an investigation into the murders since it involved a German citizen. Human rights and religious groups sounded an outcry, calling for greater freedom in Turkey for minorities. Turkish intellectuals and other leaders expressed regret for the brutal killings and tried to uncover various trends in the Turkish society that could have brought about such a violent and bloody crime on Malatya soil. Questions quickly began to emerge seeking for a connection between the Malatya killings of the three Christians and the deaths of the Catholic priest Santoro and the Armenian writer Hrant Dink. Some people continued to question the legitimacy of the missionaries and suspected dark powers behind them, agreeing that though their deaths were especially horrible and disturbing, they nevertheless had been guilty of intrigue.

In an important interview with the press, Mustafa Aydin, a retired security official, made observations about the social climate preceding the murders.

Q: When you look at the incident in Malatya, what do you see?

A: It's not just in Malatya, but many things can be seen in this kind of event and developments. In the last years we have seen a flaring up of sensitivities about missionary activity in Turkey. I believe that the activities of some elements on television, in the media and unauthorized voices have spoken about missionary work with unnecessary, deceptive, and negative purposes; these are some of the forces aggravating sensitivities. One example is how the news has been spread that there are hundreds of thousands of house churches in Turkey and that Christians number 300,000. Irresponsible and unauthorized voices are saying similar things.

Q: But for example, the Saadet Party General President Recai Kutan said that there are 32 house churches in Malatya, 34 in Eskisehir. He got this information from the Ministry of Religious Affairs.

A: I can't know that, but I estimate that there are a total of 200–300 house churches in Turkey.

Q: Another [political] party president said in a speech in 2006 that in 3.5 years 40 thousand house churches opened in Turkey.

A: That number is not in my information. We should ask for the source of this information.

Q: You worked as the Sakarya Security director. For example, after the 1999 earthquake, many foreign foundations were opened for aid purposes. Among these were missionary organizations, it was thought that some of the citizens in Sakarya become Christians.

A: After the earthquake there was a group involved in foundation activity. The greatest activity was in Sakarya. That aid had its roots in the Vatican. Because they were active in Sakarya it was thought that they were doing missionary work. I did a serious study of some units. I didn't chance to come across anything. It was thought that a husband and wife had become Christians for money. I couldn't confirm that. There's no doubt that we should be in the struggle with units who threaten the ethnic security in the country, which would break ethnic wholeness and would use religion to bring people into enmity with one another. However, freedom of religion and thought is a sensitive subject. It's important to have tolerance between religions and to have these sensitivities.

Turkish Church Leaders Press Conference

Approximately 5000 Turkish believers of Muslim background live in Turkey. They have sought to co-operate both as a matter of obedience to the command for Christian unity expressed in the New Testament and as a matter of self-identification as a religious minority in the larger context of Turkish society. The enormity of the Malatya crisis brought the risk of more "copy-cat" crimes against the struggling Christian community, perhaps pushing it to near extinction.

Just hours after the murders several Turkish church leaders from across the country agreed they needed to speak out so they hastily boarded planes, buses or cars and headed for Malatya to hold a press conference. They wanted to give a clear message to the entire observing nation of Turkey that legitimate, loyal Turkish citizens could become Christians, and these Christian citizens requested and expected under the Turkish constitution protection and equal rights with Muslim citizens. They made their statement publically, showing their faces and names openly, at no small risk to themselves, having at that time, just hours after witnessing the bloody murder of their friends and fellow believers, no reassurance that someone might not attempt the same thing on them.

A leading pastor from Ankara, Ihsan Ozbek, denounced the unprecedented torture and murder, extolling the upright character of the three men. He pointed out that Uğur's courage in his phone conversation with Gorkhan may have spared him and his wife harm or death. "These are the first martyrs, this is the first Protestant blood to flow in Turkey since 1960," he said. "We didn't want Necati, Uğur and Tilmann to die." He also commented, "Every day from the newspapers and television comes idea that missionaries plan treachery and buy people with money. This is a witch-hunt. Everyone needs to ask how this country could have created people-butchering humans ... On the day these murders happened, Turkey was buried in the darkness of the Middle Ages. For a long time the seeds of intolerance, racism and enmity toward Christians have been sown. Now these are being reaped little by little."

Bianet News reported more from Ozbek,

There are Christians who share their faith. In Malatya are Muslims who share their faith. Christians also share their faith. This is a modern country. In a modern country Christians share their faith. We are open. We want to distribute the *Injil*. Just as Muslims want to distribute the Qur'an we want to distribute the *Injil*.[13]

Correcting False Reports

While the leaders of the Turkish church were making public statements denouncing the murders and requesting greater security for themselves and their congregations scattered across Turkish cities and towns and with the attention of the other countries fixed on watching the Turkish government's response to the murders, some unethical persons looked for a way to use the story of the murders for personal advantage. They could perhaps be best described with Jesus' metaphor, "wolves in sheep's clothing." The shock and horror of the murders drew attention and sympathy from Christians in other countries, making these opportunists think they could cash in on the event. One such example is a letter that went out over email to countless Christians in America and other Western countries. The writer exaggerated the details of the murders, making a terrible situation even worse, apparently reasoning that if pity and shock could stir people to dig into their pockets, more pity and shock could make them dig deeper. The email was manipulative and deceitful, so leaders of the Turkish churches, some of the same men who addressed the press in Malatya, issued a letter correcting the misinformation and warning Christians in other countries to beware of fraudulent attempts to solicit money. The following is the text issued by the Protestant Alliance.

Alliance of Protestant Churches of Turkey

To Churches and Ministries worldwide

Dear Brothers and Sisters in Christ,

The Alliance of Protestant Churches of Turkey is the alliance of local churches within Turkey covering the full spectrum of churches throughout our country and is a full member of both the European Evangelical Alliance and the World Evangelical Alliance.

We highly regret the need for this letter, however having pondered our responsibilities before God and the church in Turkey and worldwide, we feel obliged to send this letter out on what has become a very important and unavoidable subject.

As many of you will know on 18 April 2007, the Christian community in Turkey suffered the deep tragedy of the brutal killing of three believers in the city of Malatya in Eastern Turkey. This shook us all, and both locally and internationally many reached out in prayer and support, including financial support, for the families of the victims. In such times obviously various letters of information and appeals circulate, we have had to either ignore or make some corrections on some such letters where some unintentional errors have been made. However we are extremely upset with the blatant deception of the attached report sent out by Mr. Naim Aksam of Adana Turkey, associated with Turkish Mission Ministries from Shreveport, LA/USA. The report sent out by Mr. Naim Aksam is full of lies and fabrications and we are shocked and appalled that such a tragic event has been turned into an act of self-promotion and money grabbing. We have attached the report in question as it was written and also a second copy of the same report with our comments added in red. His report is full of lies and fiction, for example his claims that he saw the bodies in the morgue and how they were mutilated are complete lies. We have the testimonies of those who actually saw the bodies (including one of the widows) and an autopsy report. Furthermore his claim for financial help for relocating the believers in Malatya is total fabrication; most of the local believers have not moved and have no intention to do so, the few believers who have moved (mainly foreigners) have done so with absolutely no need of financial support from the claimant! You will find many more deceptions in the attached report.

Some of our church leaders have warned some groups and churches in previous years against similar excesses by this person, but these warnings have sadly been ignored. The misuse of such a tragedy is the last straw for us. We therefore, as the general body of local churches in Turkey, urgently and strongly request that the report in question by Naim Aksam and related ministry are not circulated; that people, churches and ministries supporting them are warned against this falsehood. We request those who support this work to stop and thoroughly investigate what that they have innocently been donating to. We would also like to encourage everyone to make it a principle to get references for people and organisations from others in the field before and during our acts of support.

In Christ's Uniting Spirit,
Executive Committee
Chairman, General Secretary, Members[14]

Unquestionably the murders caused significant financial loss for many, especially the two women who become widows, each with small children to feed and clothe and house. Uğur's elderly parents also suffered the immense loss of a healthy son who helped support them in their final years. Universal human compassion has moved many concerned individuals to reach out to these three families over the years since the deaths. Not only local Christians, but Muslims, non-religious persons, Turks, Europeans, Asians and other nationalities have poured out material and emotional support.

Caught in the Courts

The Malatya murder court case opened in 2007. Five young Turkish men were apprehended at the Zirve crime scene April 18, 2007, their hands, clothes and shoes bloodied from beating and stabbing two Turkish and one German Christian multiple times then slitting their throats. The police arrived at the crime scene in time to arrest all five just minutes after two victims had died and the third fought bravely for life. Their knives still dripped with blood while the police handcuffed them. The case should have been open and shut. No crime could be easier to prove, no guilt could be clearer. The five men had plotted and planned, making preparations for days, weeks, perhaps months beforehand. They went into a book distribution office, tied up three unarmed, peaceful family men, systematically tortured them and then slaughtered them, nearly beheading them, like sacrificial animals.

The deed sent shock-waves of terror throughout the nation and world. But the defendants approached the court case seemingly unconcerned, even belligerent. They appeared to feel confident that persons in high places would protect them so that they wouldn't have to face any serious penalty for their crime, and certainly not the full force of the law. The reasons for their confidence began to come to light during the months the case moved forward. Investigations revealed that the murders involved a web of other people, some quite influential.

Emre Gunaydin not only survived his three-story fall trying to flee the crime scene, he eventually came out of his coma, regaining full mental and physical abilities. The confessions and evidence gathered in the period after the murders seemed to mark him as the key leader of the five men and the probable link with other plotters in a wider circle.

In May 2008 Emre was scheduled to face the court for questioning. After lunchtime the handcuffed Emre entered the courtroom surrounded by nine guards, some carrying automatic rifles. The stern and hardened military guards hovered beside the suspect with greatest care. In the middle of the nine guards, Emre stood dressed in a plaid sports coat, a dark shirt and black pants. He wore a pair of thin rimmed glasses which he took on and off several times during the questioning. He took his seat in the witness box directly facing the three judges and two prosecutors. To his right a panel of five defense lawyers sat at long tables covered with piles of documents and several computers.

To his left, more than a dozen plaintiff lawyers sat along the wall with their documents and computers. The suspect looked pale and thin, probably from having survived a three-story fall and subsequent coma then living in solitary confinement under high security. Just after arriving in the courtroom, Emre started motioning to the defense lawyers, pointing to his mouth trying to indicate he was hungry. The defense lawyers spoke back and forth with him and one another. The head judge asked about the commotion. "Your honor," they answered, "our client is hungry."

With some consternation the judge inquired, "Are you telling me he didn't have any lunch?" He looked to the leader of the military guards, "Commander, didn't the suspect eat any lunch."

"We ate sir, but he didn't have anything."

After more consultation, the chief judge said, "Then we will take a fifteen minute recess so he can eat." Once again the battery of heavily armed guards escorted Emre out of the courtroom. A little later they re-entered to resume the examination.

On the witness stand Emre brought out several hand written pages of testimony. Although he had provided a testimony a year earlier, he said he completely rejected that testimony since he had given it only twenty five days after falling three stories and going into a coma. He said the current hand written testimony was the one he wanted to officially present to the court as his personal testimony of the events related to the killings. The court secretary took the eight pages and handed them to the head judge. The judge glanced over them then asked Emre to read them out loud. The secretary passed them back to Emre. The second confession varied from the first, thus he opened himself for the accusation of perjury, not the only time that would happen.

Emre stood up and began reading. His read the paper, speaking so quickly, the chief judge had to interrupt him more than once requesting he slow down. His spoke with a voice that was a bit raspy and high pitched. In previous testimonies before the court the other four men all accused Emre of actually killing Necati, Uğur and Tilmann. In direct contradiction of the earlier statements, Emre's lengthy written testimony had one purpose: absolve him of all guilt.

He attempted to do this in three ways. First, he portrayed himself as an astute and clever observer who had unearthed the missionaries' real agenda to undermine the political and social unity of the state by setting religious sects against one another and partnering with the PKK and Israel. In his own opinion, his investigation of the missionaries was a noble attempt to protect his homeland.

Second, he accused the missionaries of saying and doing things that insulted and cursed Islam and the prophet Muhammad. Therefore, his desire to expose the missionaries was also an attempt to protect his religion. When Emre accused Necati of cursing and attacking him and his religion, the Turkish believers present in the courtroom gasped loudly. One burst out in exasperation, "Necati would never do such a thing."

Third, he tried to demonstrate his innocence by claiming he entered the Zirve offices with no intention to kill anyone. He said that the worst thing he did while in the Zirve offices was slap Tilmann and that he was in the restroom washing his hands while some of the other guys were actually knifing the three believers in the other rooms. He even said he was sorry he had been at the scene of the crime. The rehearsed testimony shrewdly turned him from a victimizer into a victim, sowing seeds of doubt about the character and intentions of Necati and the others, planting the idea in the court's mind that even though something bad had happened to the missionaries, it was something that probably just got out of hand and in any case, it was perhaps something they deserved. After helping destroy the lives of three innocent men, he then attempted to destroy their reputation, with them having no opportunity to ever again speak for themselves.

After Emre's testimony the judges and prosecutors proceeded to cross examine him. They challenged him on his claim that the missionaries were attempting to divide the land and set up a Christian empire in partnership with Israel. The chief judge asked, "Is Israel a Christian nation? How can you say they are working to set up a Christian empire here?" Later he said, "I've looked at the Christian websites you mention and I don't see anything on them suggesting the political threat you are accusing them of. The only thing I see on these Christian websites is that they are trying to say the Christian religion is good."

Emre had no answer for the judges.

The court hearing brought forth no confessions of guilt in spite of the fact that five young men were caught at an unimaginable crime scene where two believers had died from having their throats slit and a third still gasped for breath before dying hours later. All five found ways to extricate themselves. After hearing their testimonies, it seemed that no one had killed anybody, that no one had in fact died. But three men were buried in the grave, so who killed them?

A concerned observer closely followed the hearing that day and then wrote his friends around the world saying,

> Monday in court it appeared we had three murders, but no murderers. A courtroom with an impressive number of international observers and press. What will the judge do to resolve the situation? Four young men witnessed by a policeman standing at the scene of the crime with bloodied knives in their hands. But no murderers. A young man who nearly killed himself in an attempt to flee the scene of the crime. But no murderer. Where will the judge go from here with this case? So ... We continue to pray for God's intervention ...

Having sat through the tedious court hearing with Emre, one local Malatya journalist, Bulent Kutluturk, published a column the next morning posing the troubling question, "How Many People were Killed?"

> When Emre Gunaydin was taken out of the courtroom surrounded by guards front and back, he had an unchanging expression. He might have felt happy to see someone he knew, but his expression didn't change. He must not have seen anyone he knew.
>
> It's the first time I've felt sorry for a murder suspect. I saw his

being beyond help, I saw his loss of hope, and I saw that like dozens of people everything for him had finally melted away.

When Susanne Geske looked at Emre Gunaydin her expression changed with a question ... why? There was no answer and she had the expression of suffering on her face.

Suffering ... Susanne Geske and her three children, Uğur Yuksel's weeping mother, Necati Aydin's wife, and the dozens of people they knew? Among the suffering are at least fifty people directly related to the victims.

There are five suspected killers. All right, are there only three people who died? Do you think Emre is alive? The other suspects? Those close to them. How many corpses are there? Are there just three who died? This is a massacre, isn't it? How many murders were there?

 **Conspiracy
Defined**

With evidence mounting of a pattern of violent hostility against Christians across Turkey since the year 2000, plaintiff attorneys decided in August 2008 to ask the court to formally connect the Malatya murders with the Ergenekon investigation. The Ergenekon case involved numerous members of the military, government, media and mafia, apparently acting with ultranationalist and religious motives in a number of murders and other acts of violence and intimidation. These acts were allegedly supposed to foment social unrest, creating a pretext for a military coup.

In October 2009 Ramazan Akyurek, head of Turkey's police intelligence department, was removed for allegedly failing to properly do his job in providing security for the Armenian journalist Hrant Dink and the three Christians killed in Malatya. Evidence suggested that he had foreknowledge of the killers' plans but failed to act.

By late fall 2009 the case had made progress in bringing forth more evidence that the Malatya killings were indeed part of a much larger web of plots designed to create widespread social unrest in Turkey, apparently with the purpose of destabilizing the government. Lawyers for the plaintiffs openly acknowledged that the Malatya case was probably connected to the killings of Hrant Dink and the Catholic priest Santoro, but devoted their energy primarily to bringing the Malatya killers to justice, calling for three life sentences.

In 2009 as the Turkish press brought out more shocking revelations of Turkish military plans for violence against their own Turkish citizens, Turkish columnist Eyup Can wrote, "If even half of what is written in *Taraf* is accurate, everybody with a conscience in this country has to go mad ..." Turkish law enforcement officials responded quickly to the new evidence, taking dozens of military personnel and ultranationalist sympathizers into custody and initiating an investigation.

At the February 2010 hearing the prosecution requested the maximum sentence for the five men. They also stated that if the case were closed without looking further into suspected masterminds of the murders, they would seek to take the case to the Supreme Court of Appeals. The prosecution submitted a 17-page report explaining the crimes of Emre Gunaydin, Salih Gürler, Cuma Ozdemir, Hamit Ceker and Abuzer Yildirim, which included forming a terrorist organization, theft, and tying, torturing and murdering Necati, Uğur, and Tillman. The prosecution requested the court to give them each three consecutive life sentences.

March 2011 brought a stunning new development in the case when the chief Ergenekon prosecutor Zekariya Oz ordered the arrests of seven people considered the possible masterminds of the Zirve murders. Among those arrested were military officers and a theology professor.

Outside of Turkey, the European Stability Initiative produced an in-depth and balanced analysis of the Malatya murders. They produced their findings in the January 2011 report entitled, "Murder in Anatolia. Christian Missionaries and Turkish Ultranationalism." A chronology of the court hearings is included in the report, showing that by January 2011, the court had met thirty times without a verdict. Finding some hopeful trends in their analysis of the Malatya case, the ESI wrote,

> ... since the Malatya court case began in late 2007 has been a decrease in openly anti-Christian media reports. There has also been a noticeable decline in the violence targeting Christians in Turkey. This can be quantified: in recent years the Association of Protestant Churches in Turkey has published annual reports about human rights violations against Protestants.[15]

The decline of anti-Christian attacks in Turkey brought some relief and a flicker of hope to the men, women and children in Turkey and around the world who gathered in memorial services on April 18, 2011 to mourn loss of their loved ones, forgive their enemies and look to God who alone could bring justice for the wronged and redemption to the guilty.

Some years after the martyrdom a couple of younger believers, Cuma and Ester, shared their hopes. Cuma said, "The best thing I can imagine is the country becoming familiar with Jesus Christ. But among the developed countries, here is one of the highest levels of prejudice and difficulty when we try to freely explore spiritual questions, open places of worship or lift the religion category from our identification cards. So I feel that before the prejudice can start to end, there should be a new history written according to Anatolian culture taking Jesus Christ into consideration."

Ester added that she hoped, "to see Turkish Christians no longer stigmatized as traitors and enemies of the country. I hope people would see that we believe from our hearts and not for material gain or for employment. Of course what I especially would want to see is several million people accepting Jesus the Messiah as Lord. There are many other things, like the government removing the lies about Christians and Jesus from the school textbooks. I think the prejudice starts there because a child trusts everything his or her teacher says, it stays in their minds. Then people have the wrong ideas without ever studying and checking it out to find the truth. I hope that millions can investigate Jesus and seek who the Lord is."

Farhat contributed his thoughts about the future saying he hoped, "that one day all of Turkey will be free for believers in Jesus to live and explain their faith. I have this dream, but to bring the Messiah to this land and explain him we need to have the opportunity and I believe one day it is coming. Most people don't really know believers in Jesus. Christians are continuously presented as enemies and infidels. People don't even know whether Christians believe in God or not. But one day this people will know the truth about believers in the Messiah and will know the truth about the true Messiah Jesus. People will question why the bad things have happened, especially the murders in Malatya, and they will understand that the negative propaganda is false, that these things are wrong and evil. That is my dream."

 # White Robes

The most important thing for a Turk is honor.
—*Anatolian Turkish man*

Of the original twelve apostles, only John grew old and died naturally. In his final days spent in exile on the island of Patmos, a small bit of yellow rock where warm Mediterranean waters splash, he had a vision of the end of the world. He saw the divine beauty of the exalted and conquering Son of God, the power of which made him fall upon his face almost like a dead man. In the book of Revelation he bequeathed these dramatic and prophetic scenes to the generations of believers who would come afterwards. He wrote,

After this I beheld, and, lo, a great multitude, which no man could number, of all nations, and kindreds, and people, and tongues, stood before the throne, and before the Lamb, clothed with white robes, and palms in their hands; And cried with a loud voice, saying, Salvation to our God which sitteth upon the throne, and unto the Lamb.

As John watched the multitude, a heavenly personage suddenly drew near and asked him, "Who are these in white robes, where did they come from?"

John replied, "Sir, you know who they are."

The man continued, "These are they which came out of great tribulation, and have washed their robes, and made them white in the blood of the Lamb. Therefore are they before the throne of God, and serve him day and night in his temple: and he that sitteth on the throne shall dwell among them." Revelation 7:13–17

The question is worth repeating. Who are these people, the ones in the white robes? They are the countless men, women and children who died for their faith in Christ. Some who stand among them are famous, some are ordinary. Among them stands Stephen, stoned to death by an enraged mob outside of Jerusalem, just a couple of years after Jesus died on the cross. Then there is Polycarp, torched on a stake by Roman soldiers in AD 155 just outside of Smyrna, now modern Izmir. Felicity, a courageous young mother, died for Christ just after birthing her baby in AD 203. In 1316 Ramon Lull crumpled to the ground under the relentless blows of stones in a town in North Africa after patiently sharing the Gospel with Muslims for decades.

Joshua, a Native American of the Delaware tribe in central Indiana, refused to recant his faith while burning on a post before the eyes of his fellow tribesmen in 1805. And on April 18, 2007 three more men, Necati Aydin, Uğur Yuksel and Tilmann Geske departed Malatya, Turkey and took their place before the throne and the Lamb, having shed the mortal for the immortal, clothed in white robes.

The violent and untimely death of good people always raises the puzzling issue of how an all-powerful, perfectly just and fully loving God can allow such evil to continue unchecked. Was his arm too short to reach into Malatya? Is it too weak to open the eyes of Muslims to understand true nature and purpose of Jesus? Is there some obscure, hidden plan?

To ask such questions must always lead back to the person of Jesus himself, the incarnation of that same all-powerful, perfectly just and fully loving God whom we question. God himself was brutally tortured and killed. Through Jesus, God did not only enter fully into the suffering of humanity, he upended a hopeless situation.

Turning it around completely.

Turning it into a victory.

The least that can be drawn from this truth is that God does not look unfeelingly or uninterestedly upon human suffering. The greater hope that can be gained is that God will use even the most evil situations to bring his Kingdom to this world. That is the hope that the wives and friends of Necati, Uğur and Tilmann have expressed time and again. Their lives were not a waste and they will bring more to faith in Jesus Christ through their deaths than they did in life.

One sunny afternoon three years after the attack Necati's close friend Orhan sat down for tea and considered the question, if Necati could speak to us right now from heaven, what might he say? Orhan answered, "You know, I could give a very playful answer to this question because when we were together Necati and I loved to clown around and have fun. So I can imagine that the three men might say, 'You can try to keep making things hard for us, but we are at the side of the Messiah now.' It's just a lighthearted way to think about it. They fulfilled their work. They would say we should lift the banner higher because they gave their lives for the things of this land. They have passed the banner on to us and would say, 'Don't let the banner down, lift it higher.' And you know, we can't really do any more to honor them. They have the greatest honor of Jesus Christ receiving them to his side … I loved them very much …"

Endnotes

To give this book a more personal feeling and make it easier to read, it has been adapted into story form. While sources are referenced, parts of the story have been creatively dramatized while trying to stay as close as possible to the history and facts of the people and places involved.

1. www.todayszaman.com/news-108716-three-killed-in-attack-on-bible-publisher.html.

2. Jonathan Carswell with Joanna Wright, *Married to a Martyr*, p. 34, 35.

3. Name has been changed.

4. Cyrus Hamlin, *Among the Turks*, p.144.

5. Ibid. 144–145.

6. Ibid. 147.

7. Stephen Kinzer, *Crescent and Star*, 10.

8. Ibid. 62.

9. Yaşar Nuri Öztürk, *Allah Ile Aldatmak (Using God to Deceive)*, 267.

10. Carswell, p. 84.

11. Ibid. 95.

12. www.challengenews.org/showstory.php?i=2007/september&s=story_2&l=US-ES&f=

13. bianet.org/bianet/insan-haklari/94805-pastor-ozbek-hayatimiz-tehlike-altinda

14. www.worldevangelicalalliance.com/news/view.htm?id=1326

15. www.esiweb.org/index.php?lang=en&id=156&document_ID=124

Picture gallery

Malatya street bazaar

Malatya street bazaar

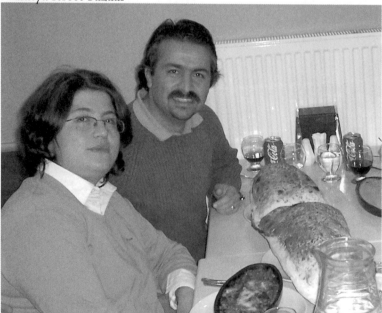

Necati and Shemse

Necati and family in 2002

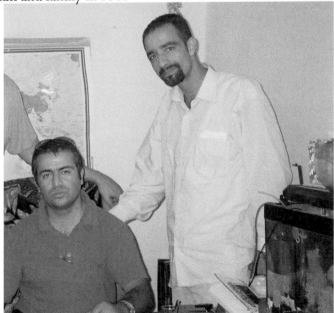

Necati and Uğur in their publishing office

Necati baptizing Uğur

Necati's family

Uğur and Tilmann on a ministry trip

Tilmann playing the guitar

Tilmann

Uğur

Necati on his motorcycle

The offices where the murders took place

Uğur's mother at his graveside